Gooseberry Patch

Country
Quick
& Easy

Fast family favorites and
nothing-to-it meals that are
simple, satisfying & delicious.

Gooseberry Patch

An imprint of Globe Pequot
64 South Main Street
Essex, CT 06426

www.gooseberrypatch.com

1•800•854•6673

Copyright 2023, Gooseberry Patch 978-1-62093-515-6

Photo Edition is a major revision of *Country Quick & Easy*.

Check out our cooking videos on YouTube!

If you spot this icon next to a recipe name, it
means we created a video for it. You'll find it at
www.youtube.com/gooseberrypatchcom.

Table of Contents

"Normal day, let us be aware of the treasure you are."-Mary Jean Irion

Dedication

For all of our country friends who love homemade cooking that's yummy as can be & easy as 1·2·3!

Appreciation

Warmest thanks to our wonderful friends for sharing their favorite quick & easy recipes... Your enthusiasm makes Gooseberry Patch so much **FUN**!

"Friendship is a sheltering tree." -Samuel Taylor Coleridge

Goodies to GO!

- ☐ Order bulbs
- ☐ Dentist!
- ☐ Thank you notes
- ☐ Baby Gift
- ☐ Garden Club
- ☐ Church program
- ☐ Return phone calls
- ☐ Dinner!

"The best thing to spend on a child is time." –Unknown

Barbecued Steak Pinwheels

Cheri Maxwell
Gulf Breeze, FL

A great quick & easy dinner before an evening soccer game.

1-lb. beef steak
1 c. barbecue sauce, divided
2 green peppers, quartered

1 onion, quartered
1 tomato, quartered
4 10-inch flour tortillas

Brush both sides of steak with half of the barbecue sauce. Place steak and vegetables on rack in broiler pan so surface of meat is 2 to 3 inches from heat source. Broil for 5 to 6 minutes per side or until desired doneness. Halfway through cooking time, slide out broiler pan and brush sides of steak with remaining barbecue sauce. Slice steak and vegetables into thin strips. Divide filling among tortillas; roll up and slice each into quarters; secure each slice with a toothpick. Makes 16 pinwheels.

Store fresh parsley in a glass of water in the refrigerator to make it last longer.

Easy Honey Drummies

Darrell Lawry
Kissimmee, FL

I've made these for Friday night football games for as long as I can remember...they're a tradition.

3 lbs. frozen chicken wings,
    thawed
1 c. honey

2 T. curry powder
1 t. ginger
1 t. cayenne pepper

Arrange wings in a single layer on an ungreased baking sheet. Bake at 400 degrees for 10 minutes. In a small mixing bowl, combine remaining ingredients until well blended. Spoon half of honey mixture over wings; bake for an additional 10 minutes. Turn wings and spoon remaining honey mixture over; bake an additional 10 minutes. Let cool slightly before serving. Makes 8 servings.

Gather your girlfriends for tea! It's the perfect way to catch up with friends or co-workers. Get together once a month at each others' houses...go ahead and stop at the bakery for some dainty cookies, too.

Pineapple & Ham Quickies

Debbie Lloyd
Newark, OH

Speedy...and tasty!

20-oz. can pineapple tidbits,
   drained

4 slices 1/4-inch thick cooked
   ham, cubed

Place a pineapple tidbit, a ham piece and an additional pineapple tidbit on toothpicks. Place on an ungreased baking sheet. Broil 3 to 4 inches from heat source for 3 to 4 minutes. Makes approximately 2 dozen appetizers.

Kielbasa Bites

Elizabeth Cyr
Wallingford, CT

Serve warm with cheese & crackers.

2 lbs. kielbasa, sliced
1 T. oil
3 to 4 T. brown sugar, packed

1 T. vinegar
3 to 5 T. orange juice

In a large skillet, fry kielbasa slices in oil until brown; drain half of the drippings. Add brown sugar, vinegar and orange juice. Cook over low heat for 40 minutes, stir occasionally. Makes approximately 7 to 8 dozen appetizers.

Removing honey from measuring cups or spoons has never been easier...just coat your spoon or cup with vegetable oil before measuring the honey.

Goodies To Go!

Pizza-Chicken Roll-Ups

Donna Nowicki
Center City, MN

Prepare a salad while these are baking...so easy!

4 boneless, skinless chicken
   breasts
12 slices pepperoni

8 slices mozzarella cheese,
   divided
15-oz. can pizza sauce
Garnish: fresh parsley, minced

Flatten chicken to 1/4-inch thick. Place 3 slices of pepperoni and one slice of cheese on each chicken breast. Roll up tightly; secure with toothpicks. Place in a greased 11"x7" baking dish. Spoon pizza sauce over roll-ups. Bake, covered, at 350 degrees for 35 to 40 minutes. Uncover and top with remaining cheese. Bake an additional 5 to 10 minutes or until cheese is melted. Sprinkle with parsley. Slice each chicken breast in quarters before serving. Makes 16 appetizers.

Is the frame too big for your picture? Use vintage fabric as a pretty backdrop.

Delightful Deviled Eggs

Robin Wilson
Altamonte Springs, FL

My family always looks forward to my special deviled eggs...especially at the holidays.

12 eggs, hard-boiled
1/2 c. Thousand Island salad dressing
salt and pepper to taste
Garnish: paprika

Slice eggs in half lengthwise. Place yolks in a small mixing bowl. Mix Thousand Island dressing with egg yolks; salt and pepper to taste. Spoon mixture into egg halves. Sprinkle top of eggs with paprika. Makes 24 eggs.

Remove water stains from vases by rubbing with a vinegar soaked paper towel.

Goodies TO GO!

Bubbly Cheese Garlic Bread

Angie Bowan
Tarpon Springs, FL

My children love this delicious bread! All ingredients can be adjusted to your taste...use a mixture of all three cheeses, if you like.

1/2 c. butter, softened
1 to 2 cloves garlic, crushed
1/2 to 1 c. creamy Italian salad
    dressing
1 loaf Italian bread, halved
    lengthwise

2 c. shredded Cheddar,
    mozzarella or Monterey
    Jack cheese
2 t. dried parsley

Blend butter, garlic and salad dressing together in a small bowl. Place bread on a baking sheet, cut-side up. Spread butter mixture over both halves. Top with shredded cheese and parsley. Bake, uncovered, at 375 degrees for 10 to 20 minutes, until cheese is melted and bubbly. Slice each half into 8 pieces; serve warm. Makes 16 servings.

For a really quick side dish, cook chopped green peppers in butter for about 5 minutes. Add canned corn and salt and simmer until golden...yummy.

Turkey & Black Bean Quesadillas

Jo Ann

Perfect for those nights when everyone is busy with homework, meetings and rehearsal.

15-oz. can black beans, rinsed
   and drained
6 oz. Cheddar cheese, cubed
4 oz. thinly sliced, cooked
   turkey, cut into strips

1/2 c. salsa
8 8-inch flour tortillas
2 T. butter, melted
Garnish: sour cream and salsa

In a large mixing bowl, stir together beans, cheese, turkey and salsa. Brush one side of tortillas with butter. Place buttered side down on an ungreased baking sheet. Spoon about 1/3 cup filling on half of each tortilla; fold in half. Bake at 375 degrees for 10 to 15 minutes or until heated through; let cool for 5 minutes. Cut each quesadilla into 3 wedges. Garnish with sour cream and salsa. Makes 24 servings.

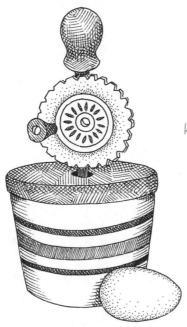

Cleaning your house while your kids are still growing is like shoveling the walk before it stops snowing.

–Phyllis Diller

Cheese-Stuffed Peppers

Jolie Newman
Yucca Valley, CA

These make a tasty appetizer for a party or potluck.

24-oz. jar whole mild banana
    peppers, drained
12-oz. carton cream cheese,
    softened

6-oz. pkg. dried, sliced salami

Cut stems off the peppers and remove seeds; rinse. Slice horizontally if needed to remove all seeds. Fill each pepper with cream cheese and wrap a slice of salami around each pepper; secure with a dab of cream cheese or a toothpick. Makes 8 whole appetizers or slice each into thirds for approximately 2 dozen appetizers.

Chicken Bites

Twila Koehn
Fruitland, ID

With only 3 ingredients, this is quick to make for a family on the move!

4 skinless, boneless chicken
    breasts, cubed
1/2 c. mayonnaise

1 sleeve round, buttery crackers,
    crushed

Toss chicken cubes in mayonnaise, then roll in crushed crackers. Place on an aluminum foil-lined baking sheet and bake at 350 degrees for 10 minutes. Turn and bake another 10 minutes or until juices run clear. Makes approximately 4 dozen appetizers.

Broiled Cheese Rounds

Tammy McCartney
Oxford, OH

Make ahead and freeze...just spread bread with bacon mixture, freeze on baking sheets. When frozen, place rounds in plastic zipping bags, thaw for one hour before baking.

1 lb. bacon, crisply cooked and crumbled
1 lb. shredded sharp Cheddar cheese

1 onion, minced
1 to 2 T. mayonnaise
2 loaves sliced party rye bread

In a medium mixing bowl, combine bacon, cheese and onion; blend in mayonnaise. Spread mixture onto bread slices; place on an ungreased baking sheet. Broil 3 to 4 inches from heat source for 3 minutes. Makes 30 appetizers.

Fabulous Franks

Cindy Watson
Gooseberry Patch

Serve with hot, spicy mustard for a little kick!

1 egg
1 T. water

1 frozen puff pastry sheet, thawed
10 hot dogs, halved

In a small mixing bowl, combine egg and water together; set aside. Unfold pastry and cut into twenty, 1/2-inch strips. Wrap pastry strips around hot dogs, pressing gently to seal. Place about 2 inches apart on an ungreased baking sheet; brush with egg mixture. Bake at 400 degrees for 15 minutes or until golden. Makes 20 appetizers.

Goodies TO GO!

Ranch Pretzel Bites

Susan Young
Madison, AL

Enjoy during your favorite movie!

16-oz. pkg. large pretzels
2-oz. pkg. dry ranch salad
   dressing mix

3/4 c. oil
1-1/2 t. garlic powder
1-1/2 t. dried dill weed

Break pretzels into bite-size pieces; place in a large mixing bowl. In a separate mixing bowl, combine remaining ingredients and pour over pretzels; toss to coat. Pour onto an ungreased baking sheet. Bake at 200 degrees for one hour; stir every 15 minutes. Makes 16 servings.

Add 20 to 30% more flavor to your cup of coffee! Simply wet the paper filter before brewing.

Bacon-Sausage Links

Mary Johnston
Attica, IN

The EASIEST appetizer for your next potluck.

1 lb. sliced bacon
16 links sausage

1 c. brown sugar, packed

Cut bacon into thirds, wrap 1/3 slice of bacon around each sausage link and secure with a toothpick. Place on an ungreased baking sheet; sprinkle with brown sugar. Bake at 350 degrees for one hour or until bacon is crisp. Makes 16 appetizers.

Garden Vegetable Spread

Michelle Campen
Peoria, IL

Use this as a sandwich spread or a delicious dip for your favorite veggies.

8-oz. pkg. cream cheese,
    softened
1/2 c. cucumber, chopped
1 carrot, shredded

1 green onion, chopped
1 t. lemon juice
1/4 t. dried dill weed

In a medium mixing bowl, combine all ingredients together. Chill before serving. Makes 1-1/2 cups.

Need to peel peaches, pears or tomatoes in a hurry?
Simply scald them in hot water, then submerge them
in cold water...the skin will peel right off.

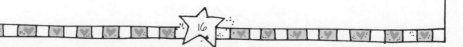

Goodies to Go!

Terrific Tuna Spread

Mary Kowaleski
Shawano, WI

Tasty little bites that can also be spooned on toasted rounds of swirled rye or crunchy celery sticks.

3 12-oz. cans tuna, drained
1 c. mayonnaise-type salad
   dressing
1-1/2 c. celery, chopped
3 T. pickle relish

salt and pepper to taste
15 dinner rolls or mini pastry
   shells

In a large mixing bowl, combine tuna, salad dressing, celery, pickle relish, salt and pepper. Spread on rolls or spoon into pastry shells. Makes 15 appetizers.

Heat lemons in the microwave for 30 seconds for twice the juice...perfect for fresh-squeezed lemonade.

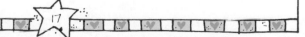

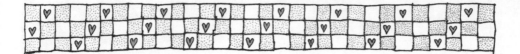

Cheeseburger Cups

Elizabeth Bevill
Helena, GA

So tasty, and the kids just love them!

12-oz. tube refrigerated biscuits
catsup and mustard to taste

1 lb. ground beef, browned
1 c. shredded Cheddar cheese

Spray muffin cups with non-stick vegetable spray. Roll out biscuits until each is big enough to fit into muffin tins with enough dough to cover. Mix together catsup and mustard with ground beef. Fill each biscuit cup with meat mixture. Sprinkle cheese over all. Fold dough over top. Bake at 425 degrees for 10 to 12 minutes or until golden brown. Makes 4 to 6 servings.

Mango-Curry Spread

Nancy Barborak
Austin, TX

Crunchy and deliciously spicy.

8-oz. cream cheese, softened
1/2 t. salt
1/2 t. curry powder
1 t. Worcestershire sauce
8 dashes hot pepper sauce

1/2 c. pecans, finely chopped
1/2 c. mango chutney
4 slices bacon, crisply cooked
    and crumbled

Blend together cheese, salt, curry, Worcestershire and hot pepper sauces together. Shape into a ball, then flatten to 1/2-inch thick. Press pecans in top of spread, spoon on chutney and sprinkle bacon on top. Serve with crackers. Makes approximately 2 cups.

To quickly rid your iron of black residue, sprinkle salt on your ironing board, turn iron setting to high and "iron" the salt until the residue is gone.

Goodies to Go!

Cheesy Ham Puffs

Lisa Miller
Lorain, OH

Make ahead to bring to a family gathering.

1 c. shredded Swiss cheese
1 c. cooked ham, diced
1 egg

8-oz. tube refrigerated crescent
rolls

In a medium mixing bowl, combine first 3 ingredients. Roll out dough and cut into 12 small squares that will fit inside mini muffin tin cups. Lightly oil muffin cups and press the square pieces of dough into each. Spoon cheese mixture into the center of each dough square. Bake at 350 degrees for 10 minutes or until knife inserted comes out clean. Makes 12 appetizers.

Terra cotta pots make great serving dishes or ice buckets! Just line them with plastic before using.

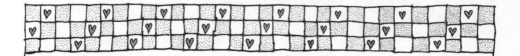

Chip Dip

Sheila Vukovich
North Canton, OH

Pick up a bag of baked potato chips to serve with this tasty dip.

8-oz. pkg. cream cheese,
   softened
2 T. milk

1/3 c. catsup
2 T. onion, chopped
2 T. French salad dressing

In a large mixing bowl, combine all ingredients together with a mixer. Refrigerate for 2 to 3 hours before serving. Makes 10 to 12 servings.

Munchable Snack Mix

Coralita Truax
Loudonville, OH

Sweet and salty...take along for a road trip snack
that everyone will enjoy.

16-oz. pkg. chocolate
   candy-coated mini baking
   bits
12-oz. can salted peanuts

11-oz. pkg. butterscotch chips
2 c. raisins
1 c. cashews

In a large mixing bowl, combine all ingredients; mix well. Place in resealable plastic bags. Makes 10 cups.

A real time-saver...double your sugar cookie recipe and freeze
some of the dough in individual plastic bags. Thaw and bake
for a quick, homemade treat.

Sausage-Spinach Pitas

Grace Jackson
Honeoye, NY

These tiny pitas make terrific bite-size tailgate appetizers.

1 lb. ground Italian sausage
10-oz. pkg. frozen, chopped
  spinach

2 c. shredded mozzarella cheese
1/8 t. nutmeg
12 small pita bread pockets

In a large skillet, thoroughly cook sausage, add spinach and cook until spinach is thawed; drain. Add cheese and nutmeg; toss. Spoon into pita pockets and place them on an ungreased baking sheet. Bake at 350 degrees for 20 minutes or until hot. Makes 12 pitas.

When hard-boiling eggs, add a pinch of salt to the water to keep the shells from cracking.

Hot Pepper Bites

Diana Krol
Nickerson, KS

Serve hot or cool...either way they're great!

8-oz. pkg. cream cheese,
   softened
4 slices bacon, crisply cooked
   and crumbled
1/2 t. chili powder

1/4 t. garlic powder
2 lbs. banana peppers, seeded
   and halved
1 c. seasoned bread crumbs

In a large mixing bowl, blend together cream cheese, bacon, chili powder and garlic powder. Stuff each pepper half with the cream cheese mixture; roll in bread crumbs. Place peppers in a greased jelly roll pan. Bake at 350 degrees for 30 minutes or until golden. Makes approximately 2 dozen appetizers.

Use an old drawer to make a handy shelf. It's so easy...perfect for kitchen spices or the guest bath.

Party Tortilla Wraps

Mandy Hardy
Middleville, MI

My favorite "quick" recipe.

4 10-inch flour tortillas
8-oz. pkg. chive cream cheese
1-lb. sliced cooked ham

8-oz. pkg. shredded American
   cheese

Lay out tortillas; spread with cream cheese. Place several slices of ham on each tortilla; sprinkle with cheese. Roll up tortillas. Place in refrigerator for 15 minutes. Cut vertically into one-inch pieces. Makes 40 appetizers.

Store cheese in a zipping bag...plastic wrap gives an "off" flavor and aluminum foil won't keep it from drying out.

Hot Chicken Sandwiches

Brenda Smith
Monroe, IN

Sandwiches in the slow cooker...so easy.

28-oz. can cooked chicken,
  undrained
2 10-3/4 oz. cans cream of
  chicken soup

4 T. grated Parmesan cheese
7 slices bread, toasted and cubed
24 dinner rolls

In a large mixing bowl, combine all ingredients together, except hamburger buns, and place into a 5-quart slow cooker for 3 hours. Spread chicken mixture on rolls. Makes 24 sandwiches.

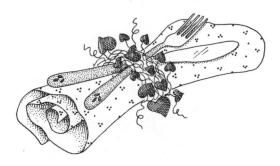

Hot Parmesans

Fay Nielsen
Walkerton, IN

Sure to please at any potluck.

1 loaf sliced party rye bread
1 onion, minced
1 c. mayonnaise

3/4 c. grated Parmesan cheese
1/8 t. Worcestershire sauce

Place bread slices on a baking sheet in a single layer. Mix together onion, mayonnaise, cheese and Worcestershire sauce; spread on bread. Broil 3 to 4 inches from heat source for 3 to 4 minutes or until toasted. Makes 15 servings.

Bacon Swirls

Irene Robinson
Cincinnati, OH

Serve these warm for the best flavor.

8-oz. tube refrigerated crescent
    rolls
3-oz. pkg. cream cheese,
    softened
5 slices bacon, crisply cooked
    and crumbled

2 T. onion, minced
1 t. milk
grated Parmesan cheese to taste

Separate rolls into 4 rectangles; press perforations to seal. In a mixing bowl, stir together cream cheese, bacon, onion and milk; spread on dough. Roll up jelly roll-style, starting at the long side; press edges to seal. Cut each roll into 8 pieces and place on an ungreased baking sheet. Sprinkle with Parmesan cheese. Bake at 375 degrees for 12 to 15 minutes or until lightly browned. Makes 2-1/2 dozen appetizers.

*Vintage carry-alls are terrific for corraling clutter.
Pick up a few to use in the kitchen, craft room
or on a buffet table.*

Sausage Squares

Liz Sulak
Bryan, TX

Just the right size to nibble on at your next family reunion.

2 c. shredded Cheddar cheese
1/2 lb. ground sausage,
   browned

2 eggs, beaten
1 c. biscuit baking mix
1 c. milk

Place cheese in the bottom of a greased 9"x9" baking dish. Sprinkle sausage over the cheese. Combine eggs, baking mix and milk. Pour over sausage mixture. Bake, uncovered, at 350 degrees for 45 to 50 minutes or until golden brown. Cut into bite-size squares. Makes 8 to 10 appetizers.

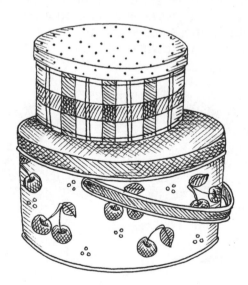

Pack a plastic container of frozen lemonade or iced tea with your lunch in the morning to keep food chilled. When you're ready to enjoy your sandwich, you'll have a frosty drink as well!

Goodies TO GO!

Bacon-Wrapped Water Chestnuts

Sharon Neylon
Middleton, MA

The best snack for family game night...it's so easy to serve.

1/4 c. soy sauce
1 T. brown sugar, packed

8-oz. can whole water chestnuts, drained
10 slices bacon

In a small mixing bowl, mix soy sauce and brown sugar until sugar dissolves and mixture is well blended. Stir in water chestnuts and marinate for 15 minutes; stir occasionally. Line a baking sheet with aluminum foil. Cut bacon slices in half crosswise. Wrap each water chestnut with a bacon slice; secure with a toothpick and arrange on ungreased baking sheet. Bake at 400 degrees for 15 minutes. Makes 30 appetizers.

Hot Seafood Spread

Kara Allison
Dublin, OH

Make an edible serving bowl! Just hollow out a round loaf of sourdough bread and spoon seafood spread inside.

2 8-oz. pkgs. cream cheese, softened
2 c. flaked crab
2 T. green onions, finely chopped

1/2 c. prepared horseradish
1/2 c. sliced almonds
paprika to taste

In a large mixing bowl, beat cream cheese until smooth. Blend in remaining ingredients except almonds and paprika. Spread mixture into an ungreased 9" pie plate. Top with almonds and sprinkle with paprika. Bake, uncovered, at 375 degrees for 20 minutes. Makes 3 cups.

Caramel-Apple Dip

Brenda Harrell
Beulaville, NC

A quick & easy dip...perfect to bring to autumn gatherings!

8-oz. pkg. cream cheese,
   softened
1/4 c. honey
1/2 c. caramel ice cream topping

1/4 t. cinnamon
3 to 4 green apples, cored and
   sliced

In a medium serving bowl, combine cream cheese, honey, caramel topping and cinnamon; beat until smooth. Store in refrigerator until chilled. Serve with apple slices. Makes 2 cups.

A great way to keep brown sugar from hardening is to drop a slice of fresh apple in the bag...it absorbs extra moisture.

Incredible Mini Burger Bites

Megan Besch
Omaha, NE

My family adores these...yours will too! We make them for football parties and summer get-togethers.

2 lbs. lean ground beef
1-1/2 oz. pkg. onion soup mix
2 eggs, beaten
1/2 c. dry bread crumbs
3 T. water
1/2 t. garlic salt
1 t. pepper

24 dinner rolls, split
6 slices American cheese,
   quartered
Garnish: catsup, mustard,
   shredded lettuce, thinly
   sliced onion, dill pickles

Mix first 7 ingredients in a bowl; refrigerate for an hour. Spread meat mixture over a greased large baking sheet. Cover with plastic wrap and roll out evenly with a rolling pin. Discard plastic wrap; bake at 400 degrees for 12 minutes. Slice into 24 squares with a pizza cutter. Top each roll with a burger square, a cheese slice and desired garnishes. Makes 24 mini sandwiches.

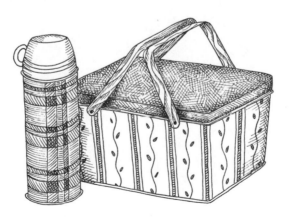

Packing cupcakes for lunch? Slice them in half and place the bottom of the cupcake on the frosted piece. That way, icing won't stick to your plastic bag.

Nanny's Stuffed Celery

Dawn Mills
Falls Church, VA

This recipe is a family tradition started by my grandmother in the 1940s. She always brought it to our holiday dinners.

1-1/2 c. chopped walnuts
1 c. green olives, chopped and
   2 T. juice reserved
2 8-oz. pkgs. cream cheese,
   softened

1/4 c. milk
2 bunches celery, chopped into
   2-inch pieces

In a small mixing bowl, combine walnuts and olives. In a large bowl, blend cream cheese and walnut mixture; add milk and olive juice. Mix thoroughly with a fork. Stuff each celery piece with filling. Let chill one hour before serving. Makes 4 dozen appetizers.

Lemon verbena is an easy herb to grow and tastes great with peaches and strawberries.

Triple-Take Grilled Cheese

Abigail Smith
Worthington, OH

Delicious in winter with a steaming bowl of tomato soup. And delicious in summer with produce fresh from the garden!

1 T. oil
8 slices sourdough bread
1/4 c. butter, softened and
　divided
4 slices American cheese
4 slices Muenster cheese

1/2 c. shredded sharp Cheddar
　cheese
Optional: 4 slices red onion,
　4 slices tomato,
　1/4 c. chopped fresh basil

Heat oil in a skillet over medium heat. Spread 2 bread slices with one tablespoon butter; place one slice butter-side down on skillet. Layer one slice American, one slice Muenster and 2 tablespoons Cheddar cheese on bread. If desired, top with an onion slice, a tomato slice and one tablespoon basil. Place second buttered bread slice on top of sandwich in skillet. Reduce heat to medium-low. Cook until golden on one side, about 3 to 5 minutes; flip and cook until golden on the other side. Repeat with remaining ingredients. Makes 4 sandwiches.

*A bee is never as busy as it seems...
it's just that it can't buzz any slower.*

-Kim Hubbard

BLT Dip

Barbara Thurman
Carlyle, IL

Serve with bread rounds...sure to please.

1 lb. bacon, crisply cooked and
    crumbled
1 c. mayonnaise

1 c. sour cream
2 tomatoes, chopped

In a medium serving bowl, blend together bacon, mayonnaise and sour cream. Add tomatoes just before serving. Makes 2-1/2 cups.

Dried Beef Cheese Ball

Sharon Hall
Delaware, OH

My famous "secret ingredient" recipe for the yummiest cheese ball ever!

2 8-oz. pkgs. cream cheese,
    softened
1 c. shredded Cheddar cheese
2-1/2 oz. pkg. dried beef, finely
    chopped and divided
3 T. green onion, chopped

2 to 3 T. mayonnaise-style
    salad dressing
1 t. Worcestershire sauce
1/2 c. chopped walnuts
assorted snack crackers

Combine all ingredients except walnuts and crackers, setting aside 1/4 cup chopped beef. Blend well and form into a ball. Mix nuts and reserved beef; roll cheese ball in mixture to coat. Wrap in plastic wrap; chill 3 to 4 hours. Serve with crackers. Makes one cheese ball.

Looking for an easy picnic table centerpiece? Simply set a yellow votive in the center of a pretty sunflower...beautiful!

Super Nachos

Mary Murray
Mt. Vernon, OH

So quick...makes a great snack or even lunch!

2 10-inch flour tortillas
3/4 c. salsa
4-oz. can green chilies, drained
   and diced

1/2 c. sliced black olives
1 c. shredded Monterey Jack
   cheese

Place tortillas on an ungreased baking sheet; spread salsa over tortillas. Sprinkle chilies and olives over the salsa; top with cheese. Bake at 425 degrees for 10 minutes or until the tortillas are crisp and the cheese is melted. Use a pizza cutter to slice each in 8 wedges. Makes 8 appetizers.

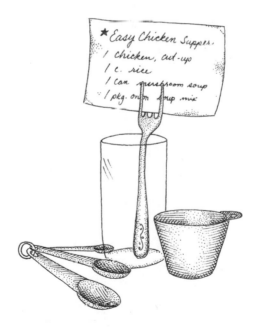

Create a quick recipe card holder! Place a fork, tines up, in a glass. Slip in your recipe card and it will be held cleverly in place.

High Rollers ▶

Michelle Sheridan
Huntsville, AL

*A new flavor twist on the familiar tortilla roll-ups we all love.
Try honey-roasted turkey too...delightful!*

6 12-inch flour tortillas
2 8-oz. containers honey-nut
   cream cheese spread
3 c. baby spinach leaves
9-oz. pkg. deli oven-roasted
   turkey slices

6-oz. pkg. sweetened dried
   cranberries
Optional: seedless grapes

For each roll-up, spread a tortilla with 2 tablespoons cream cheese.
Layer with spinach leaves; add 2 slices turkey to cover most of
spinach. Spread another tablespoon cream cheese over turkey; sprinkle
with one to 2 tablespoons cranberries. Roll up tightly; secure with a
toothpick. Place tortilla rolls seam-side down on a tray; cover and chill
for one to 2 hours. At serving time, trim off ends of rolls; slice 1/2-inch
thick. Garnish with grapes, if desired. Makes about 5 dozen.

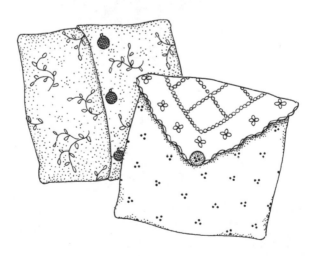

*Your favorite meatloaf won't stick to the bottom of the
loaf pan if you lay a slice of bacon in first.*

Goodies TO GO!

Dill Dip

Kristine Silva
Fairview, PA

Serve with fresh vegetables.

1 c. sour cream
1 c. mayonnaise
1-1/2 T. dried parsley flakes
1-1/2 T. dried, minced onion

1/4 t. dried dill weed
1/2 t. celery salt
1/2 t. seasoned salt flavor
   enhancer

In a medium serving bowl, blend all ingredients together; chill. Makes 10 to 15 servings.

Fruit Smoothy Dip

Linda Bair
Springfield, OH

Yummy with oranges, apples, pears, or kiwi.

2 c. sour cream

1/4 c. orange juice

In a small serving bowl, combine sour cream and orange juice together. Refrigerate at least 30 minutes. Makes 8 to 10 servings.

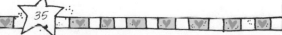

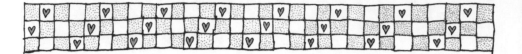

Cinnamon Puffs

Margaret Schaefer
Fairview Park, OH

A quick treat for the kids.

8-oz. pkg. cream cheese
1 egg yolk
1/2 c. plus 2 T. sugar, divided
1 t. vanilla extract

1 loaf sliced white bread, crusts
   removed
1 T. cinnamon
1 c. butter, melted and cooled

In a medium mixing bowl, blend together cream cheese, egg yolk,
2 tablespoons sugar and vanilla extract. Roll bread slices flat; spread
filling on bread. Roll up jelly roll-style. Combine remaining sugar
and cinnamon in a small mixing bowl. Dip bread in butter, then
in sugar-cinnamon mixture. Place on baking sheets and freeze. When
frozen, cut each roll into 3 pieces. Bake at 350 degrees for 15 minutes.
Makes 45 bite-size pieces.

Add a drop of bleach to your fresh-from-the-garden bouquet
to keep it beautiful and long-lasting.

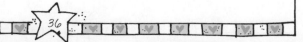

Goodies TO GO!

Open-Faced Sandwiches

Judy Fowler
Mesquite, TX

So easy to serve at a buffet.

1 lb. ground beef, browned
1 onion, chopped
1 lb. bacon, crisply cooked and
    crumbled

10-3/4 oz. can tomato soup
1 c. pasteurized process cheese
    spread, cubed
8 hamburger buns

In a large mixing bowl, combine all ingredients together, except buns; spoon mixture onto tops and bottoms of buns. Place on an ungreased baking sheet. Bake at 400 degrees for 10 minutes. Makes 16 open-faced sandwiches.

Keep an eye on yard sales for old picture frames to use as serving trays. Attach handles and a piece of glass for the tray. Decoupage pictures or postcards onto the glass to make it your very own.

Shrimp Puffs

Tori Willis
Champaign, IL

My daughter always asks me for these when she's having sleepovers. Of course, I have to double the recipe!

1/4 c. grated Parmesan cheese
1/4 c. mayonnaise
2 T. green onion, minced
1/4 t. garlic powder

2-1/2 oz. can cocktail shrimp,
   drained
5 slices white bread

In a small mixing bowl, mix cheese, mayonnaise, onion and garlic powder together until blended; stir in shrimp. Cut ten, 2-inch rounds from bread slices. Mound one tablespoon of the shrimp mixture onto each bread round. Place on an ungreased baking sheet. Bake at 375 degrees for 10 to 12 minutes or until golden brown. Makes 10 puffs.

Ham Dip

Debbie Schmidt
Broken Arrow, OK

Serve with crispy crackers for a tasty appetizer.

5-oz. can cooked ham
2 8-oz. pkgs. cream cheese

green onion, chopped to taste

In a large mixing bowl, combine all ingredients together. Makes 15 to 20 servings.

Goodies To Go!

Zesty Meatballs

Melissa Langnes
Waterford, MI

These are so easy...the slow cooker does all the work.

1 c. catsup
1 c. grape juice
1 c. apple jelly

1 c. tomato sauce
5 lbs. frozen meatballs

In a 6-quart slow cooker, combine catsup, grape juice, apple jelly and tomato sauce. Simmer on low one hour, stirring occasionally until ingredients are well blended. Add meatballs. Cook on low for 4 to 5 hours. Makes 30 servings.

Keep ground meat, cooked or uncooked, in the refrigerator for two to three days at the most. Write the date on the container and remember, "When in doubt, throw it out."

Pizza Crescent Snacks

Beth Flack
Terre Haute, IN

Make a buffet with all the fixings and let everyone create their own pizza.

8-oz. tube refrigerated crescent
   rolls
14-oz. jar pizza sauce

3/4 c. sliced pepperoni
3/4 c. sliced mushrooms
1 c. shredded mozzarella cheese

Unroll crescent rolls onto an ungreased baking sheet into individual triangles. Spread a layer of pizza sauce on dough and top with pepperoni and mushrooms. Sprinkle cheese on top; roll up into crescent shape. Bake at 375 degrees for 18 to 25 minutes or until rolls are golden brown and cheese is bubbling. Makes 8 appetizers.

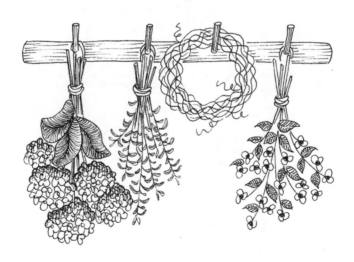

Baking soda can bring out the natural sweetness of tomato sauce by reducing the acid. Add about 1/4 teaspoon per quart of sauce as it simmers.

Cucumber Sandwiches

Vicki Rawlins
Mundelein, IL

So easy and it makes enough for the soccer team!

8-oz. pkg. cream cheese, softened
1 c. mayonnaise
1-oz. pkg. dry Italian salad dressing mix

1 loaf sliced party rye bread
1 cucumber, thinly sliced
dried dill weed to taste

In a medium mixing bowl, blend together cream cheese, mayonnaise and dressing mix. Spread half of bread slices with cream cheese mixture and top each with a cucumber slice. Sprinkle with dill weed and top with remaining bread slices; chill until ready to serve. Makes 40 to 50 sandwiches.

Out of your favorite wood polish? Whip up your own with four parts vegetable oil and one part lemon juice; mix well. The oil will moisturize your wood and the lemon juice will clean and leave a fresh fragrance!

Mom's Ham Barbecue

Barbara Obaker
Gibsonia, PA

A warming meal for an autumn night.

1 lb. thinly sliced, boiled ham	1 onion, chopped
2 T. butter	2 T. brown sugar, packed
1/2 c. catsup	1 T. vinegar
1/2 c. water	16 mini hamburger buns

Heat ham in a large skillet with butter. In a medium mixing bowl, combine remaining ingredients, except buns; mix in with ham. Simmer for 15 minutes. Serve on buns. Makes 16 sandwiches.

Santa Fe Mini Tacos

Lesley Baker
Rexburg, ID

Our favorite tried-and-true family recipe.

1 lb. ground beef	1-1/4 oz. pkg. taco seasoning
15-1/4 oz. can corn, drained	1 doz. mini taco shells
15-1/2 oz. can kidney beans, rinsed and drained	Garnish: sour cream and shredded Cheddar cheese

In a large skillet, brown ground beef; drain. Add corn and beans to the ground beef mixture; blend in seasoning. Place ground beef mixture in taco shells. Serve with sour cream and cheese. Makes one dozen mini tacos.

Sandwiches are so tasty in flour tortillas and pitas...and a lot less messy!

Meals in Minutes

☐ Call Mom

☐ Work out

☐ School snacks

☐ Car Pool

☐ Piano Lessons

☐ Soccer Practice

☐ Dry Cleaning

☐ Dinner!

"Life is not so short; there is always time for courtesy." – Ralph Waldo Emerson

Bacon-Burger Skillet Dinner

Myrna Streb
Dalton, OH

A satisfying meat and potatoes meal from the heart of Amish country.

6 slices bacon, halved
4 1/4-lb. ground beef patties
salt and pepper to taste
1 onion, sliced

6 potatoes, sliced
4 carrots, sliced
1/2 t. dried parsley
1/4 c. water

Line the bottom of a large skillet with bacon; place beef patties over bacon. Season with salt and pepper. Place onion over patties. Cover onion with potatoes; add carrots. Sprinkle all with parsley. Cook on medium-high heat until bacon sizzles; add water, cover and cook on low heat for 20 to 25 minutes; flip burgers. Cook an additional 20 to 25 minutes, stirring occasionally, or until bacon is crispy and vegetables are tender. Makes 4 servings.

Shells & Sausage

Danette Varble
Marengo, IL

Serve with warm, crusty bread...so yummy!

14-oz. pkg. shell macaroni and
cheese, cooked
13-oz. pkg. smoked sausage,
chopped

10-3/4 oz. can cream of
mushroom soup
10-oz. pkg. frozen, chopped
broccoli, cooked

In a 5-quart slow cooker, combine macaroni and cheese, sausage, soup and broccoli. Cook on low for one to two hours, or until heated through. Makes 4 to 6 servings.

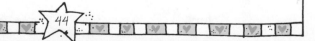

Ham & Swiss Casserole

Lauren Klein
Savannah, GA

Set a basket of warm rolls on the table and glasses of cold milk...your family will come even before you call them!

8 oz. sour cream
12-oz. pkg. shredded Swiss
cheese, divided

8-oz. pkg. macaroni, cooked
3 c. cooked ham, chopped

In a small mixing bowl, combine sour cream and 3/4 of cheese together. In a lightly greased 13"x9" baking dish, place macaroni and ham. Add sour cream mixture to baking dish; stir until blended. Top with remaining cheese. Bake, uncovered, at 350 degrees for 30 minutes or until bubbly. Makes 6 to 8 servings.

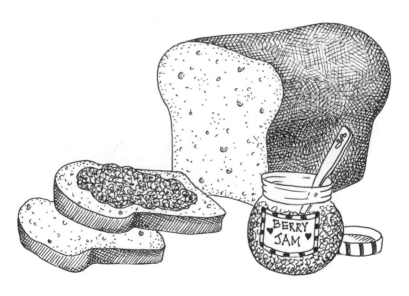

To give your warm-from-the-oven bread a sweet, shiny glaze, brush with honey...it also absorbs moisture and bread will stay fresh longer.

Pork Chop Casserole

Lisanne Miller
York, ME

Boneless chicken breasts can be substituted for pork.

4 pork chops
pepper to taste
4 T. orange marmalade
6-oz. pkg. stuffing mix, cooked

15-1/4 oz. can corn, drained
4 c. instant mashed potatoes,
  cooked
1/2 stick butter, sliced

Place pork chops in a 13"x9" baking dish coated with non-stick vegetable spray. Season with pepper and add marmalade. Spread stuffing over pork chops; top with corn. Spoon mashed potatoes over all; dot with butter. Bake, uncovered, at 375 degrees for 25 minutes; cover and bake an additional 20 minutes. Makes 4 servings.

Making your favorite casserole? Make an extra to freeze.
Enjoy the next time you need a quick dinner!

Molly Bee's Tex-Mex Casserole

Molly Langham
Houston, TX

For a really spicy taste use hot salsa!

2-lb. pkg. frozen hash browns
2 lbs. ground beef
16-oz. jar salsa

1 c. shredded sharp Cheddar cheese

Cook hash browns according to package directions and place in an ungreased 13"x9" baking dish. In a large skillet, brown ground beef; drain. Pour salsa over beef and cook for 10 minutes, stirring occasionally. Place beef mixture into the middle of the hash browns. Sprinkle cheese over all. Bake, uncovered, at 350 degrees for 20 minutes. Makes 6 to 8 servings.

Hold a true friend with both your hands.
–Proverb

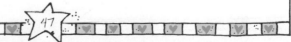

Hamburger Bundles

Julie Whiteside
Queenstown, MD

Make your cooking time even less by preparing the stuffing mix according to the microwave directions.

10-3/4 oz. can cream of
   mushroom soup
1/4 c. milk
1 lb. ground beef

1 T. catsup
2 t. Worcestershire sauce
6-oz. pkg. stuffing mix, cooked

In a medium mixing bowl, blend together soup and milk. In a large mixing bowl, combine beef, catsup and Worcestershire sauce. Divide mixture and shape into 4 patties. Place 1/4 cup of stuffing onto each patty and draw sides up to make a ball. Place in an ungreased 13"x9" baking dish; cover with soup mixture. Bake, uncovered, at 350 degrees for 35 to 45 minutes. Makes 4 servings.

Add freshly-snipped herbs such as dill weed, basil, or thyme to biscuit dough for delicious variety.

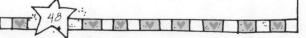

Meals in Minutes

Quick Pizza Casserole

Michelle Wittenberg
Long Beach, CA

The great taste of pizza in a casserole.

6-oz. pkg. shell macaroni,
   cooked
8-oz. jar pizza sauce
8-oz. carton cottage cheese
4-oz. pkg. shredded mozzarella
   cheese

4-oz. pkg. sliced pepperoni,
   halved
1/2 c. onion, chopped
1/2 t. dried basil
1 T. grated Parmesan cheese

In a 2-quart microwave-safe dish, combine all ingredients except
Parmesan cheese; blend well. Sprinkle Parmesan cheese over top.
Cover and microwave on high for 7 to 9 minutes. Makes 4 to
6 servings.

*Add a pinch of cinnamon to coffee grounds before
brewing...reduces bitterness and adds
a touch of spice.*

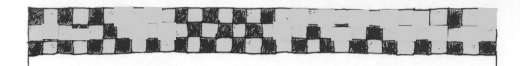

Sausage & Potato Casserole

Megan Heep
Chicago, IL

Enjoy breakfast at dinnertime! Add a platter of pancakes
and syrup for a complete supper.

1/4 c. oil
1/2 c. all-purpose flour
2 t. salt
1/4 t. pepper
4 c. milk

8 to 10 potatoes, boiled and
  sliced
1 lb. ground sausage, browned
1 c. shredded American cheese

Combine oil, flour, salt and pepper in a large skillet. Cook and stir
over medium heat until hot. Whisk in milk, stirring constantly, until
thickened; remove from heat. Layer half of potatoes, flour mixture
and sausage into an ungreased 13"x9" baking dish; repeat layers.
Sprinkle cheese on top. Bake, uncovered, at 350 degrees for
30 minutes or until cheese begins to brown slightly. Makes
8 to 10 servings.

Make a tasty butter log using fresh
herbs from the garden.
Cream together butter,
chives and shallots,
shape into a log and
wrap in wax paper;
refrigerate until firm.
Roll in herbs and serve.

HERBS

Meals in Minutes

Mexican Egg Bake

Nadine Watson
Aurora, CO

Just right served with a side of refried beans.

12 corn tortillas, torn
16-oz. can green chili sauce
16-oz. pkg. shredded Cheddar
   cheese, divided

6 eggs
Garnish: sour cream, lettuce,
   shredded and tomato,
   chopped

Layer tortillas, chili sauce and 3/4 of cheese into an ungreased 13"x9" baking dish. Break eggs over top, spacing evenly. Sprinkle with remaining cheese. Bake, uncovered, at 350 degrees for 30 to 40 minutes. Slice into squares and garnish with sour cream, lettuce and tomato. Makes 8 to 10 servings.

Cheesy Macaroni & Beef

Jean Silva
Epsom, NH

Garlic bread and a crisp salad make this a meal.

1 to 1-1/2 lbs. ground beef
14-oz. can stewed tomatoes,
   drained
26-oz. jar spaghetti sauce

2 7-1/4 oz. pkgs. macaroni and
   cheese, cooked
8-oz. pkg. shredded mozzarella
   cheese

In a large skillet, brown ground beef; add tomatoes and spaghetti sauce. Combine macaroni and ground beef mixture into an ungreased 13"x9" baking dish; sprinkle with cheese. Bake, uncovered, at 350 degrees for 20 minutes. Makes 4 to 6 servings.

Scattering bay leaves on pantry shelves keeps insects away.

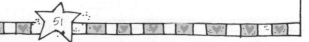

Slow Cooker Ribs

Susan Young
Madison, AL

Simmer in the slow cooker while you're out raking leaves or working in the garden.

2 lbs. pork spareribs
1 T. oil
2 onions, sliced

1-1/2 c. barbecue sauce
water to taste

Divide ribs into serving size pieces. In a large skillet, brown ribs in oil over medium-high heat; reserve drippings. Transfer ribs to a 3-quart slow cooker. Sauté onions in drippings until tender; place in slow cooker. Cover meat and onions with barbecue sauce; dilute sauce with a little water during cooking time. Cover and simmer on low for 6 to 8 hours. Makes 4 servings.

A quick gift! Give a jar of your homemade preserves with two loaves of freshly-baked bread wrapped in a pretty linen towel.

Parmesan Baked Chicken

Samantha Starks
Madison, WI

Prep time is only about 5 minutes!

1/2 c. mayonnaise-type salad dressing
1/3 c. grated Parmesan cheese
3/4 t. garlic powder

4 boneless, skinless chicken breasts
3/4 c. Italian bread crumbs

In a medium mixing bowl, combine salad dressing, cheese and garlic powder. Coat chicken with mayonnaise mixture and cover each with bread crumbs. Arrange chicken on an ungreased baking sheet. Bake at 425 degrees for 20 to 30 minutes or until lightly golden and juices run clear. Makes 4 servings.

...Steady as a clock, busy as a bee and cheerful as a cricket.

–Martha Washington

Simple Quiche

Julie Miller
Columbus, OH

Toss in green peppers, mushrooms or black olives for added flavor.

3 slices bacon, crisply cooked
    and crumbled
1 c. shredded Cheddar cheese
1/2 c. onion, chopped
4 eggs

2 c. milk
1/2 c. biscuit baking mix
1/2 t. salt
1/8 t. pepper

Sprinkle bacon, cheese and onion in the bottom of a greased 9" pie plate. In a medium mixing bowl, beat eggs and milk together; add remaining ingredients and mix until well combined. Pour into pie plate over bacon mixture. Bake, uncovered, at 350 degrees for 50 to 55 minutes or until center tests done. Let stand 5 to 10 minutes before cutting into wedges. Makes 8 servings.

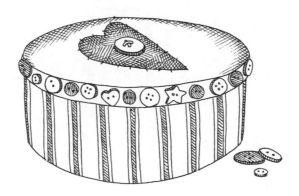

Store eggs in their cartons to prevent them from absorbing odors from other foods...preferably in the coldest part of the fridge rather than the door.

Busy Mom Lasagna

Aimee Gutowski
Fort Smith, AR

So simple...just layer in the slow cooker.

1 lb. ground beef
1/2 c. onion, diced
16-oz. jar spaghetti sauce
4 oz. cream cheese, softened
4 oz. sour cream

12-oz. pkg. wide egg noodles,
   uncooked
1-1/2 c. shredded mozzarella
   cheese
1-1/2 c. shredded Cheddar
   cheese

In a large skillet, brown beef with onion; drain. Add spaghetti sauce, cream cheese and sour cream; mix well. Coat a 5-quart slow cooker with non-stick vegetable spray. Layer the slow cooker with part of the noodles, beef mixture and cheeses. Repeat layers as necessary until cooker is full. Cover and cook on high for 2 hours, reduce heat to low for an additional 3 hours. Makes 6 to 8 servings.

Pasta with Roasted Vegetables

Vickie

Use your family's favorite vegetables to make this dish special!

1 lb. fresh mixed vegetables,
   chopped
salt and pepper to taste
2 t. dried rosemary
2 t. dried thyme

2 T. olive oil
1/2 lb. rigatoni, cooked
2 t. balsamic vinegar
2-1/2 T. grated Parmesan cheese

Arrange vegetables in a lightly greased 13"x9" baking dish. Season with salt, pepper, rosemary and thyme; pour oil over all and toss. Roast vegetables in a 500 degree oven for 10 minutes or until browned. Drain vegetables, reserving juice; set aside. In a large serving bowl, toss pasta, vegetables, reserved juice and vinegar together. Sprinkle with Parmesan cheese; toss. Makes 4 servings.

Easy Turkey Pot Pie

Kathy Miller
Easton, PA

An irresistible way to turn leftover turkey into a meal.

1-1/2 c. frozen mixed corn, peas and carrots
1-1/2 c. cooked turkey, chopped
2 10-3/4 oz. cans cream of chicken soup

1 c. biscuit baking mix
3/4 c. milk
1 egg

In an ungreased 9" pie pan, place vegetables, turkey and soup. In a medium mixing bowl, combine remaining ingredients and pour them into the pan; stir. Bake, uncovered, at 400 degrees for 35 minutes. Makes 8 servings.

Lemon Pepper Fish

Liz Plotnick-Snay
Gooseberry Patch

A scrumptious, light dinner.

1 lb. frozen cod, thawed
16-oz. pkg. frozen stir-fry vegetables
salt to taste

1 t. lemon pepper
1 t. dried rosemary
1 c. tomato juice
2-1/2 T. grated Parmesan cheese

Line a 13"x9" baking dish with aluminum foil. Place cod in dish and cover with vegetables. Season with salt, lemon pepper and rosemary. Pour tomato juice over all; sprinkle with Parmesan cheese. Bake at 400 degrees for 20 to 25 minutes or until fish flakes and vegetables are tender. Makes 4 servings.

Use a cotton rag moistened with lemon juice to dust your plants' leaves...so simple.

Mini Meat Loaves

Roxanne Bixby
West Franklin, NH

For extra special fun, use cookie cutters to shape the meat, then simply place them on a cookie sheet to bake.

1 lb. ground beef
1 onion, chopped
2 slices bread, cubed

1 egg
10-3/4 oz. can vegetable soup

In a large mixing bowl, combine all ingredients. Shape into 12 equal portions and place into ungreased muffin tins. Bake at 350 degrees for 15 to 20 minutes. Makes 6 servings.

*Make your own delicious frosty fruit pops...it's easy!
Slice your favorite fruit and combine with fresh juice.
Pour into small cups and set in the freezer. When partially
frozen, insert popsicle sticks, then freeze until firm.*

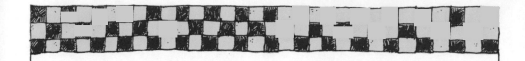

Bacon Florentine Fettuccine

Barbara Adamson
Oviedo, FL

This is incredibly simple and so fast to prepare.

16-oz. pkg. fettuccine, uncooked
2 10-oz. pkgs. frozen, creamed
  spinach
1/2 lb. bacon, crisply cooked and
  chopped

1/8 t. garlic powder
1/2 c. plus 2 T. grated Parmesan
  cheese, divided
pepper to taste

Prepare fettuccine as directed on package; drain, reserving 3/4 cup of cooking liquid. Return fettuccine and reserved liquid to the saucepan. Microwave spinach as directed on package. Add spinach, bacon and garlic to saucepan. Transfer to a serving dish and stir in 1/2 cup cheese. Season with pepper and sprinkle with remaining cheese. Makes 4 servings.

For a great seasoning, squeeze fresh lemon juice on your cooked vegetables instead of salt.

Chicken Burritos

Karen Wright
Arnold, MO

If you're really short on time, use canned chicken instead.

3 to 4 boneless, skinless chicken breasts, cooked and shredded
1-1/2 c. salsa, divided
1 c. sour cream

8 10-inch flour tortillas
10-3/4 oz. can cream of chicken soup
2 c. shredded Mexican-blend cheese

Combine chicken, 1/2 cup salsa and sour cream. Spoon chicken mixture into tortillas, roll up and place in an ungreased 13"x9" baking dish. Blend together soup and remaining salsa; pour over chicken. Bake, uncovered, at 350 degrees for 30 minutes. Sprinkle on cheese and bake an additional 5 minutes, or until cheese is melted. Makes 4 to 6 servings.

Hero Burgers

Kathleen McHale
Colonial Beach, VA

We've been making this dish for 35 years and still love it.

1-1/2 lbs. ground beef
10-3/4 oz. can tomato soup
1/3 c. onion, finely chopped
1 T. mustard
1 T. Worcestershire sauce
1 t. prepared horseradish

1 t. salt
1 loaf French bread, halved lengthwise and toasted
2 tomatoes, sliced
2 c. shredded Cheddar cheese

Thoroughly combine first 7 ingredients. Spread mixture on bottom half of bread, covering edges completely. Broil 4 to 5 inches from heat source for 10 to 12 minutes. Top with tomatoes and cheese; broil for 5 additional minutes or until cheese is melted. Cover with top half of bread. Cut into 3-inch slices and serve. Makes 4 servings.

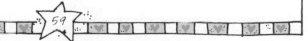

Quick Chicken & Noodles

Whitney Walsh
Yermo, CA

Perfect on a chilly night...so cozy.

49-1/2 oz. can chicken broth
10-oz. can cooked chicken,
   drained
1/2 stick butter
1/2 onion, diced

garlic powder to taste
Italian seasoning to taste
salt and pepper to taste
12-oz. pkg. extra wide egg
   noodles, uncooked

In a large stockpot, combine broth, chicken, butter, onion and seasonings; simmer over medium heat for 10 minutes or until onion is tender. Increase heat to boiling, add noodles and cook for 15 to 20 minutes or until noodles are tender. Makes 6 to 8 servings.

Hollow out a round loaf of pumpernickel bread to serve your chicken & noodles in...a quick and savory meal.

Tuna Jackstraws Casserole

Cathy Laughlin
Wichita, KS

From oven to table in no time!

4-oz. can shoestring potatoes,
    divided
10-3/4 oz. can cream of
    mushroom soup

7-oz. can tuna, drained
6-oz. can evaporated milk
4-1/2 oz. can sliced mushrooms,
    drained

Combine 3/4 of potatoes, soup, tuna, milk and mushrooms in a
greased 13"x9" baking dish. Sprinkle remaining potatoes on top.
Bake, uncovered, at 375 degrees for 25 minutes. Makes 6 servings.

Time-saver! Prepare your casserole the night before, cover
and refrigerate. Be sure to add 15 to 20 minutes
to the cooking time.

Cottage Pie

Kathy Grashoff
Ft. Wayne, IN

Perfect for after ice skating...so warm and hearty.

6 T. butter, divided
1 c. onion, diced
1-1/2 lbs. ground beef
salt and pepper to taste

1/4 t. dried savory
1 c. canned brown gravy
2 c. instant mashed potatoes,
   cooked

Heat 4 tablespoons butter in a large skillet. Add onion and cook over medium heat, stirring frequently, until tender and lightly golden. Add ground beef, salt, pepper and savory; cook for 5 minutes. Stir in the gravy and heat until bubbling. Spoon mixture into a greased 2-quart baking dish. Spread mashed potatoes over top of meat and dot with remaining butter. Bake, uncovered, at 400 degrees for 15 to 20 minutes or until potatoes are lightly browned. Makes 4 servings.

Chicken Pasta

Elizabeth Andrus
Gooseberry Patch

A nice light supper that everyone in my family can agree on.

1 lb. boneless, skinless chicken
   breasts, cubed
2 4.8-oz. pkgs. herb and butter
   angel hair pasta, cooked

10-oz. pkg. frozen, chopped
   broccoli, thawed

In an electric skillet, brown chicken on medium heat for 20 minutes. Add pasta and broccoli. Heat on low for 10 minutes or until heated through. Makes 6 servings.

Cheesy Beef & Bacon Burger Meatloaf Kelly Masten
Hudson, NY

*Growing up in a large family, we ate a lot of meatloaf.
This recipe always kept us coming back for more!*

1 lb. bacon, crisply cooked,
    crumbled and divided
1-1/2 lbs. ground beef sirloin
1-1/2 c. shredded Cheddar
    cheese
2 eggs, beaten
1/3 c. bread crumbs

1/3 c. mayonnaise
1 T. Worcestershire sauce
1/2 t. salt
1/2 t. pepper
1/2 c. catsup
1/4 t. hot pepper sauce
3 T. Dijon mustard

Set aside 1/2 cup bacon for topping. Combine remaining bacon,
ground beef, cheese, eggs, crumbs, mayonnaise, Worcestershire sauce,
salt and pepper in a large bowl; set aside. Mix together catsup, hot
sauce and mustard; set aside 3 tablespoons of mixture. Add remaining
catsup mixture to beef mixture; blend well. Press into an ungreased
9"x5" loaf pan; spread reserved catsup mixture over top and sprinkle
with reserved bacon. Bake, uncovered, at 350 degrees for 50 to
60 minutes, until done. Remove from oven; let stand 5 to 10 minutes
before slicing. Serves 6 to 8.

*It's so easy to make your own bread crumbs. Dry out slices
of fresh bread in a 250 degree oven, then tear into sections
and pulse in your food processor or blender.*

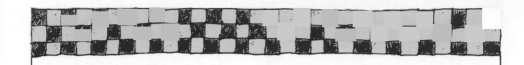

Cavatini

Bobbi Kress
Bagley, WI

Serve with garlic bread for a complete Italian meal.

1 lb. ground Italian sausage
1 lb. ground beef
salt and pepper to taste
26-oz. plus 16-oz. jar spaghetti
  sauce
3 c. spiral, elbow and small shell
  macaroni, cooked

2 lbs. shredded mozzarella
  cheese
2-1/2 oz. pkg. sliced pepperoni,
  halved

In a large skillet, brown sausage and ground beef with salt and pepper; drain. In an ungreased 13"x9" baking dish, layer half of spaghetti sauce, meat, pasta, cheese and pepperoni; repeat layers. Bake at 350 degrees for 45 minutes. Makes 8 to 10 servings.

Place candles in the refrigerator for several hours before burning to help reduce drips and make them burn longer.

Vickie's Tomato Pie

Vickie

I love to use heirloom tomatoes in this pie...red, orange, yellow, even purple! This pie smells incredible baking in the oven and tastes just like summertime.

9-inch pie crust
4 tomatoes, chopped and divided
1 onion, chopped and divided
10 to 12 leaves fresh basil, chopped and divided

1 c. shredded mozzarella cheese
1 c. shredded Cheddar cheese
1 c. mayonnaise
1/2 c. grated Parmesan cheese

Place crust in a 9" pie plate and set on a baking sheet. Bake at 400 degrees for about 12 minutes, until lightly golden; cool. Place tomatoes between paper towels to absorb as much moisture as possible. Layer half of tomato, half of onion and half of basil in pie crust; repeat layers. Mix mozzarella and Cheddar cheeses with mayonnaise; spread mixture over pie. Top with Parmesan cheese. Return pie plate to baking sheet; cover edge of crust with aluminum foil. Bake at 350 degrees for 50 to 60 minutes. Let stand 15 minutes before slicing. Makes 6 servings.

Give your kitchen a quick face-lift with vintage door pulls.

Chicken Enchilada Casserole

Shirley Alvarado
Bryan, TX

A tasty south-of-the-border dish.

4 boneless, skinless chicken
   breasts, cooked and cubed
2 10-3/4 oz. cans cream of
   chicken soup

1 c. milk
10-1/2 oz. pkg. tortilla chips
4-oz. can green chilies, drained
1 c. shredded Cheddar cheese

In a large mixing bowl, combine chicken, soup and milk together; set aside. In an ungreased 13"x9" baking dish, layer tortilla chips, half of chicken mixture, green chilies and cheese; repeat layers ending with cheese. Bake, uncovered, at 350 degrees for 25 minutes or until cheese is bubbly. Makes 8 to 10 servings.

To keep salt from clogging in the shaker, add 1/2 teaspoon of uncooked rice.

Turkey-Rice Casserole

Loretta Droege
Jerseyville, IL

Top with a sprinkling of Cheddar cheese for added taste.

10-3/4 oz. can cream of
  mushroom soup
10-3/4 oz. can cream of
  celery soup
1-1/2 c. milk

1-1/2 oz. pkg. dry onion soup
  mix
1 c. white rice, cooked
2 to 3 c. cooked turkey, cubed

Combine all ingredients in an ungreased 2-quart baking dish. Bake, covered, at 350 degrees for 35 minutes; uncover, and bake an additional 10 minutes. Makes 4 to 6 servings.

Cheeseburger & Fries Casserole

Tracy House
Nichols, NY

The kids love this recipe...it's so much fun!

2 lbs. ground beef
10-3/4 oz. can golden
  mushroom soup

10-3/4 oz. can Cheddar cheese
  soup
20-oz. pkg. frozen French fries

Brown ground beef; drain. Stir in soups and pour into an ungreased 13"x9" baking dish; arrange French fries on top. Bake, uncovered, at 350 degrees for 50 to 55 minutes. Makes 6 to 8 servings.

Black Bean Pasta

Teri Williams
Lynnwood, WA

A nice change of pace...meatless and very quick to make.

1 lb. linguine, cooked
15-1/2 oz. can black beans,
    drained, rinsed and heated

salsa to taste
Garnish: sour cream, peanuts
    and green onions, sliced

Place 1/4 of pasta on 4 plates; top with 1/4 of the beans. Spoon salsa diagonally across the beans; add a dollop of sour cream and sprinkle generously with peanuts and green onions. Makes 4 servings.

Crunchy Chicken Casserole

Kendra Keierleber
Lubbock, TX

So crunchy and cheesy...always a hit!

6-oz. pkg. wild rice, uncooked
14-1/2 oz. can French-style
    green beans, drained
10-3/4 oz. can cream of chicken
    soup
1/2 c. mayonnaise
4 boneless, skinless chicken
    breasts, cooked

8-oz. can water chestnuts,
    drained and sliced
1 oz. slivered almonds
2 c. shredded mild Cheddar
    cheese

Cook rice 5 minutes less than directed on package; mix with remaining ingredients, except cheese. Pour into a greased 13"x9" baking dish. Top with cheese. Bake at 350 degrees for 30 minutes. Makes 4 servings.

Cornbread Bake

Mitzi Pruitt
Anderson, IN

Serve with sour cream or butter.

2 7-oz. boxes cornbread mix, divided
1 lb. ground beef, browned
14-1/2 oz. can green beans, drained

1 c. frozen hash browns
14-1/2 oz. can corn, drained
1 c. shredded Cheddar cheese

Prepare one box cornbread mix as directed on package. Pour into the bottom of a greased 8"x8" baking pan. Bake at 350 degrees for 10 minutes. Combine ground beef, green beans, hash browns, corn and cheese; pour over baked cornbread mix. Prepare remaining cornbread mix as directed on package and pour over the ground beef mixture. Bake, uncovered, at 350 degrees for 25 to 30 minutes. Makes 6 servings.

*The best way to make children good
is to make them happy.*

-Oscar Wilde

Easy Italian Chicken with Pasta

Erin Tingle
Ephrata, PA

Perfect for dinner guests, easy enough for any night!

4 boneless, skinless chicken
   breasts
1/4 c. grated Parmesan cheese,
   divided
2 t. Italian seasoning

2 T. garlic powder
6 oz. angel hair pasta, cooked
26-oz. jar spaghetti sauce,
   heated

In a broiler pan, place chicken breasts and sprinkle with half of the cheese, Italian seasoning and garlic powder. Broil for 5 to 10 minutes; turn chicken breasts and sprinkle with remaining cheese, Italian seasoning and garlic powder. Broil for an an additional 5 to 10 minutes or until tests done. Serve chicken over top of pasta and pour sauce over all. Makes 4 servings.

*Mash your favorite fruit and mix with cottage
or ricotta cheese for a tasty spread.*

Homesteader's Casserole

Roxanne Bixby
West Franklin, NH

This dish has everything that you need for a balanced supper.

9-oz. pkg. frozen green beans, thawed
8-oz. can small, whole onions, drained
1 T. chopped pimento

1 lb. sausage links, cooked
3 c. instant mashed potatoes, cooked
1/2 lb. pasteurized process cheese spread, sliced

In a large mixing bowl, combine beans, onions and pimento. Layer half of the sausage, half of the potatoes and half the cheese in a 2-quart baking dish coated with non-stick vegetable spray. Layer on remaining potatoes, green bean mixture, remaining sausage and cheese. Bake, covered, at 350 degrees for 30 minutes. Makes 4 to 6 servings.

Run out of catsup? Make your own! Combine one cup tomato sauce with 1/2 cup sugar and 2 tablespoons vinegar. Mix well before serving.

Shepherd's Pie

Dale Evans
Frankfort, MI

My daughters are both married teachers, so this is the perfect quick & easy recipe...and their husbands love it.

2 lbs. ground beef
1 onion, diced
6-oz. pkg. frozen corn, thawed

10-3/4 oz. can cream of
   mushroom soup
4 c. instant mashed potatoes,
   cooked

In a large skillet, brown ground beef; drain and add onion and corn. Thoroughly blend in soup and warm through. Serve over mashed potatoes. Makes 8 servings.

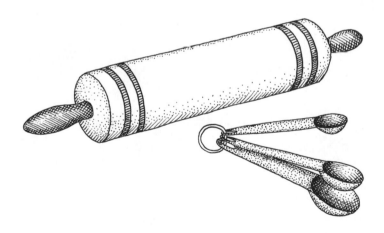

For a mock shepherd's pie in minutes, just substitute a can of cream of celery soup and frozen hash browns for the mashed potatoes...less fuss and just as tasty!

Meals in Minutes

Country Chicken Bake

Shan Walker
Blackshear, GA

The absolute tastiest way to serve chicken.

4 boneless, skinless chicken
   breasts, cubed
1/4 t. seasoned salt
1/4 t. pepper

6-oz. pkg. stuffing mix, cooked
1 c. milk
10-3/4 oz. can cream of chicken
   soup

In a medium skillet, sauté chicken with seasoned salt and pepper until juices run clear when chicken is pierced. Place chicken and stuffing in an ungreased 13"x9" baking dish. Combine remaining ingredients and pour over chicken mixture. Cover baking dish with aluminum foil and bake at 350 degrees for 10 minutes; remove aluminum foil and bake an additional 5 minutes. Makes 4 servings.

Stroganoff Skillet

DeNeane Deskins
Marengo, OH

Time-tested and so delicious.

1 lb. ground beef
1 onion, chopped
10-3/4 oz. can cream of
   mushroom soup

1 c. sour cream
1 c. beef broth
1/2 c. water
3 c. wide egg noodles, uncooked

In a large skillet, brown ground beef and onion over medium heat. Gradually blend in remaining ingredients. Bring to a boil; reduce heat. Cover and simmer for 10 minutes or until noodles are tender. Makes 4 to 6 servings.

Freeze homemade mashed potatoes in individual muffin cups. Once they're frozen, pop them out, store in plastic freezer bags and just microwave as needed.

Country Bean Casserole

Leona Toland
Baltimore, MD

The brown sugar gives this dish a subtle, sweet flavor that's so good.

1/2 lb. ground beef
1/2 lb. bacon, chopped
1 c. onion, chopped
16-oz. can pork and beans
15-1/2 oz. can lima beans,
   drained

16-oz. can kidney beans,
   drained
1/2 c. catsup
1/2 c. brown sugar, packed
1 t. salt
1 T. mustard
2 t. vinegar

Brown ground beef, bacon and onion in a large skillet over medium to medium-high heat. Add remaining ingredients, stir well then pour into an ungreased 2-1/2 quart baking dish. Bake, covered, at 350 degrees for 40 to 45 minutes or until bubbly. Makes 8 to 10 servings.

Hot Chicken Salad

Cheryl Hambleton
Delaware, OH

It's chicken salad in a casserole...yummy!

3 to 4-lb. whole fryer chicken,
   cooked and cubed
2 c. celery, sliced
1 c. sliced almonds
1 c. mayonnaise

1 t. lemon juice
salt and pepper to taste
12-oz. pkg. shredded Cheddar
   cheese

Combine first 6 ingredients in an ungreased 13"x9" baking dish. Top with cheese, then bake, uncovered, at 350 degrees for 45 minutes. Makes 6 to 8 servings.

Honey-Pecan Pork Cutlets

Kathy Grashoff
Fort Wayne, IN

You won't believe that something so good could be so simple.

1 lb. boneless pork loin cutlets
1/2 c. all-purpose flour
3 T. butter, divided

1/4 c. honey
1/4 c. chopped pecans

Pound pork to 1/4-inch thickness; coat with flour. Heat one tablespoon butter in a large skillet over medium heat. Add pork and sauté about 5 to 6 minutes or until brown on both sides. In a small mixing bowl, soften remaining butter and mix with honey and pecans; add to skillet, stir gently. Cover and simmer for 7 to 8 minutes or until juices run clear. Remove to a serving platter and spoon sauce over pork. Makes 2 to 3 servings.

To thicken gravy, add a few instant potato flakes.
It will be hearty and extra yummy.

Old-Fashioned Blueberry Pancakes

Sharon Sorrels
Troutville, VA

Breakfast for dinner! When breakfast foods are so good, you shouldn't have to just eat them in the morning. Pair these pancakes with some hashbrowns and sausage for a tasty country meal!

2 c. milk
2 eggs, beaten
1/2 c. sour cream
2 c. all-purpose flour
2 T. baking powder

2 T. sugar
1/2 t. salt
1/4 c. oil
1 c. blueberries

Combine milk, eggs and sour cream; beat well. Stir together flour, baking powder, sugar and salt; add to milk mixture. Beat until lumps disappear; mix in oil. Fold in blueberries; pour 1/4 cup batter per pancake onto a greased hot griddle. Flip when bubbles appear. Serves 4 to 6.

Vegetable sprays now come in different flavors. Use olive oil for sautéing and butter-flavor for baking pans.

Pot Roast & Veggies

Michelle Thornton
Surry, NH

Prep time is just a few minutes!

3 to 4-lb. pot roast
4 potatoes, chopped
6 carrots, chopped
1 onion, chopped

10-3/4 oz. can cream of
   mushroom soup
1-1/2 oz. pkg. dry onion soup
   mix
2 T. water

Line a 13"x9" baking dish with aluminum foil; place roast in dish. Place vegetables around roast. In a medium mixing bowl, combine mushroom soup and onion soup mix; pour over roast and sprinkle with water. Cover with an additional piece of aluminum foil. Bake at 300 degrees for 4 hours. Makes 6 to 8 servings.

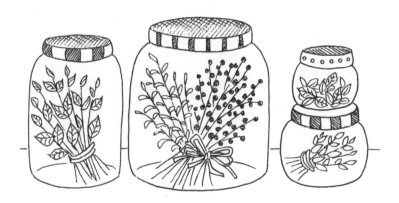

Combine two teaspoons garlic powder and a teaspoon each of dried basil, oregano and lemon juice for a no-salt seasoning for meats and vegetables.

Ranch Chicken

Sheri Davis
Maryville, TN

Steamed rice is the perfect side dish for this chicken.

1 T. margarine
4 boneless, skinless chicken
   breasts

2 c. ranch salad dressing,
   divided

In a large skillet, melt margarine. Place chicken in skillet over medium heat. Pour 1/2 of the dressing over chicken, allow breasts to brown slightly before turning over. Coat the other side of chicken with remaining dressing. Cover and reduce heat to simmer for 10 to 15 minutes, or until chicken juices run clear. Makes 4 servings.

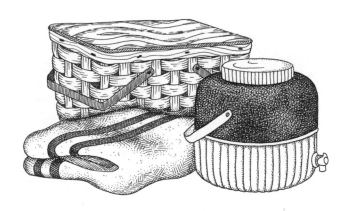

Did you know...a small bunch of mint placed in the middle of your picnic table or blanket will keep those pesky bees away?

Meals in Minutes

Easy Garlic & Herb Shrimp

Mary Bettuchy
Duxbury, MA

Especially good with warm slices of French bread.

2 lbs. cooked shrimp, peeled and
   deveined
1 c. oil
1 t. celery salt

1 t. paprika
1 t. dried basil
1 t. dried oregano
1 t. dried, minced garlic

Layer shrimp on the bottom of an ungreased 13"x9" baking dish. In a small mixing bowl, combine oil, celery salt, paprika, basil, oregano and garlic. Pour mixture over shrimp. Broil 4 to 5 inches from heat source on low heat for 5 to 10 minutes or until shrimp are bright pink and hot. Makes 6 to 8 servings.

Quick Salmon Patties

Deborah Early
Charlotte, NC

The salmon makes this dish perfect for supper, lunch or brunch.

15-oz. can salmon, cleaned and
   2 T. juice reserved
1 egg
1/3 c. celery, minced

1/2 c. all-purpose flour
1-1/2 t. baking powder
2 T. oil

In a medium mixing bowl, combine salmon, egg and celery until mixed thoroughly; stir in flour. In a small mixing bowl, combine baking powder and reserved juice; stir into salmon mixture and form into 6 patties. In a large skillet, fry patties in oil for 3 to 5 minutes per side or until golden brown. Makes 6 patties.

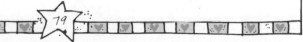

Mandarin Pork Chops

Susan Young
Madison, AL

A terrific dinner party recipe...it's simple and quick,
but tastes like you spent hours on it.

4 to 6 pork chops
1 T. oil
11-oz. can mandarin oranges,
    drained

1/2 t. ground cloves
1/8 t. pepper

In a large skillet, brown pork chops in oil for 3 to 5 minutes per side.
Top with oranges; sprinkle with cloves and pepper. Cover and cook
over medium heat for 15 minutes or until juices run clear. Makes 4 to
6 servings.

you are
my sunshine

Don't judge an orange by its skin. Pick the best by testing their
firmness and how heavy they are for their size.

Glazed Corned Beef

Claire Bertram
Lexington, KY

A terrific slow cooker recipe.

4 to 5-lb. corned beef brisket
2-1/2 T. mustard
2 t. prepared horseradish

2 T. red wine vinegar
1/4 c. honey

In a 5-quart slow cooker, cover brisket with water. Cover and cook on low for 10 to 12 hours or until tender. Place corned beef in an ungreased 13"x9" baking dish. In a small mixing bowl, combine mustard, horseradish, vinegar and honey; baste beef. Bake, uncovered, at 400 degrees for 20 minutes or until brisket browns; baste occasionally. Makes 4 servings.

It is admirable for a man to take his son fishing, but there is a special place in heaven for the father who takes his daughter shopping.

–John Sinor

Baked Fish with Parsley

Laura Strausberger
Roswell, GA

Choose a white fish, such as halibut or sole, for the best taste.

1 lb. fish fillets
1/2 c. butter, melted
2 T. lemon juice
1/4 c. onion, minced

1-1/2 t. Worcestershire sauce
1/4 t. salt
1/4 t. dried parsley

Place fillets in a lightly greased 13"x9" baking dish. In a small mixing bowl, blend together remaining ingredients and pour over fish. Bake, uncovered, at 350 degrees for 30 minutes. Makes 4 to 5 servings.

Quick Salisbury Steak

Alma Meyers
Guernsey, WY

Add a side of mashed potatoes for a hearty, filling dinner.

1 lb. ground beef
1-1/2 oz. pkg. dry onion soup
  mix

2 eggs, beaten
2 10-3/4 oz. cans golden
  mushroom soup

In a large mixing bowl, combine ground beef, soup mix and eggs; form into 4 patties. Place patties in an ungreased 13"x9" baking dish. Cover with soup. Bake at 350 degrees for 35 minutes. Makes 4 servings.

Root Beer Ham

Deborah Fletcher
Spokane, WA

Place in the slow cooker before church...perfect for a Sunday lunch.

5 lb. cooked ham   2-ltr. bottle root beer

Place ham in a 6-quart slow cooker and pour root beer over ham until covered. Cover and cook on low for 3 to 4 hours. Makes 24 to 26 servings.

Fill a basket with pine cones for a quick & easy fireside display.

No Fuss Chicken

Leanne Hockman
Bend, OR

*Rice topped with the extra sauce from the chicken is
a terrific side dish.*

8-oz. bottle Russian salad
   dressing
1/3 c. apricot preserves
1-1/2 oz. pkg. dry onion soup
   mix

6 to 8 boneless, skinless chicken
   breasts

In a medium mixing bowl, blend together dressing, preserves and soup
mix; set aside. Place chicken in an ungreased 13"x9" baking dish;
pour preserve mixture over chicken. Bake, covered, at 350 degrees for
20 minutes. Uncover and baste chicken with sauce. Cook an
additional 20 minutes. Makes 6 to 8 servings.

BBQ Chicken Pizza

Debbie Dimmer
Valley Center, CA

Guaranteed party pleaser!

2 c. boneless, skinless chicken
   breasts, cooked and
   shredded
1/2 to 1 c. barbecue sauce

1 prebaked pizza crust
1 red onion, sliced
1 green pepper, sliced
1 c. shredded mozzarella cheese

In a large mixing bowl, combine chicken with barbecue sauce; spread
over pizza crust. Arrange onion and pepper over chicken. Sprinkle
cheese over all. Bake at 450 degrees for 10 to 12 minutes, or until
cheese is melted. Makes 6 to 8 servings.

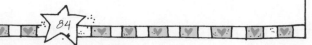

Slow Cooker Beef & Gravy

Susan Young
Madison, AL

I shared this with my friend because she loves recipes with 5 or less ingredients. This one fits the bill.

2 to 2-1/2 lb. boneless round
   steak
10-3/4 oz. can cream of
   mushroom soup

2 1-1/2 oz. pkgs. dry onion
   soup mix
1/2 to 3/4 c. water

Divide steak into serving pieces and place into a 6-quart slow cooker. In a medium mixing bowl, combine soup, soup mixes and water; pour over steak. Cover and cook on low for 7 to 8 hours. Makes 6 to 8 servings.

To easily remove burnt or stuck-on food from your skillet, simply add a few drops of dish soap and enough water to cover the bottom of pan and bring to a boil.

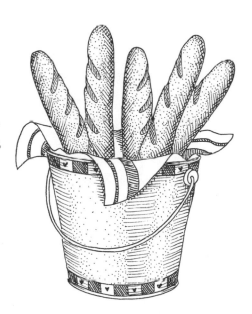

Turkey & Broccoli Alfredo

Wendy Jacobs
Idaho Falls, ID

Add fresh biscuits for a well-rounded meal.

6-oz. pkg. fettuccine, uncooked
2 c. frozen, chopped broccoli
10-3/4 oz. can cream of
    mushroom soup

1/2 c. milk
3/4 c. grated Parmesan cheese
3 c. cooked turkey, cubed
1/8 t. pepper

Prepare fettuccine according to package directions. Add broccoli in the last 5 minutes of cooking; drain. In a large skillet over medium-high heat, mix soup, milk, cheese, turkey, pepper and fettuccine mixture; cook until warm, stirring often. Makes 4 servings.

Look for an
old market basket
on wheels...it's
a clever
way to tote
your large
garden tools.

State Fair Pork Chops

Heather Denk
Naperville, IL

First prize winner!

2 eggs
1/4 c. mustard
1/4 c. brown sugar, packed

1/3 c. red wine vinegar
8 pork chops
seasoned salt to taste

In a small mixing bowl, beat together eggs and mustard. In a separate small mixing bowl, dissolve brown sugar in vinegar; add to egg mixture. Brush both sides of pork chops with brown sugar mixture and place into a greased 13"x9" baking dish. Sprinkle with seasoned salt; grill 10 minutes on each side or until juices run clear when pierced with a fork, basting at least once more during grilling time. Makes 6 to 8 servings.

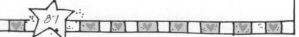

Apple cider punch! Combine 4 cups of cider with one quart vanilla ice cream and 2 cups lemon-lime soda.

Cran-Basa

Beth Bergeron
Kingston, MA

My dad has been working on the cranberry bogs since he was small. When I asked him what he thought this sauce was made of, he had no idea!

2 16-oz. cans jellied cranberry
sauce

2 16-oz. pkgs. kielbasa,
chopped
2 T. brown sugar, packed

In a medium saucepan, heat cranberry sauce over medium heat, stirring often until smooth. In a large skillet over medium heat, fry kielbasa until heated thorough and browned on all sides. Combine cranberry sauce with kielbasa; continue to heat for about 10 minutes. Stir in brown sugar and mix well. Makes 16 servings.

Deodorize cutting boards by rubbing with a paste of baking soda and water.

Autumn Apple Dinner

Elizabeth Brookshire
Parkville, MD

So warm and cozy on an autumn evening.

2 to 3 red apples, cored and
    chopped
1 onion, chopped

16-oz. pkg. kielbasa, coarsely
    chopped

Place apples and onion in a large saucepan; add kielbasa. Cook over medium heat for about 20 to 30 minutes. Makes 4 servings.

Quick Tuna Casserole

Gloria Robertson
Midland, TX

Under thirty minutes from start to finsh!

1-1/2 c. elbow macaroni, cooked
10-3/4 oz. can cream of
    mushroom soup
6-oz. can tuna, drained

5-oz. can evaporated milk
1/2 c. shredded Cheddar cheese
1/3 c. onion, chopped
3 c. potato chips, crushed

Combine all ingredients, except potato chips, in an ungreased 9"x9" baking dish; top with potato chips. Bake, uncovered, at 425 degrees for 15 minutes. Makes 4 servings.

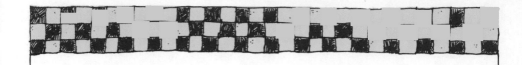

Onion Casserole

Dawn Psik
Aliquippa, PA

If you're an onion-lover, get ready for a treat!

5 onions, sliced
12 round, buttery crackers,
   crushed
1 lb. ground sausage

2 10-3/4 oz. can cream of
   mushroom soup
1/2 t. seasoned salt
1/2 c. shredded Cheddar cheese

Coat a 13"x9" baking dish with non-stick vegetable spray. Layer bottom of dish with half of the onions, crackers, sausage, remaining onions and soup. Sprinkle with seasoned salt and top with cheese. Bake, uncovered, at 400 degrees for one hour or until cheese is melted. Makes 4 to 6 servings.

Sift flour only when using cake flour. For general baking, just stir the all-purpose flour, spoon lightly into a measuring cup and level off.

Ham & Egg Casserole

Gale Willy
Star City, IN

This unusual recipe is a favorite at our house. Since we seldom eat a big breakfast, we have it for supper instead.

1/2 t. onion powder
5 eggs, hard-boiled and chopped
10-3/4 oz. can cream of chicken
   soup
1/4 c. milk

2 c. shredded Cheddar cheese
1 c. cooked ham, cubed
12-oz. tube refrigerated biscuits,
   baked

In a medium mixing bowl, combine onion powder, eggs, soup, milk and cheese; blend well. Place mixture into a greased 8"x8" baking dish. Spread ham evenly over top. Bake, uncovered, at 350 degrees for 25 minutes. Serve over biscuits. Makes 4 to 6 servings.

Make-Ahead Brunch Casserole

Kelly Dalton
Lewisburg, TN

What a time-saver...you make this casserole the night before.

1 T. butter
2 onions, chopped
2 c. sliced mushrooms
4 c. frozen hash browns, thawed
salt and pepper to taste
1/4 t. garlic salt

1 lb. bacon, crisply cooked
4 eggs
1-1/2 c. milk
1/8 t. dried parsley
1 c. shredded Cheddar cheese

In a medium skillet, melt butter and sauté onions and mushrooms until tender. Place hash browns in the bottom of a greased 13"x9" baking dish. Sprinkle with salt, pepper and garlic salt. Top with bacon, onions and mushrooms. In a medium mixing bowl, beat eggs with milk and parsley, pour over casserole and top with cheese. Cover and refrigerate overnight. Bake at 400 degrees for one hour or until set. Makes 4 to 6 servings.

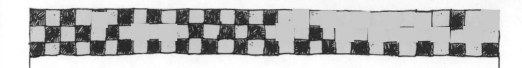

Scalloped Chicken

Ellen Forney
Ravenna, OH

Pick up a roasted chicken from the grocery store to save time.

3 to 4 c. cooked chicken, chopped
10-3/4 oz. can cream of mushroom soup

2 c. round, buttery crackers, crushed and divided
2 T. butter, melted

In a lightly greased 2-quart baking dish, combine chicken, soup and 1/2 cup crackers. Combine remaining crackers with butter and sprinkle over top of chicken mixture. Bake at 350 degrees for 40 minutes. Makes 4 to 6 servings.

Vintage tin containers and baskets are great for storing everything from dish cloths to clothespins.

Meat & Potato Pie

Punki Gehring
Allyn, WA

Sounds a little different...but definitely worth a try.

1/2 lb. ground beef
1/2 lb. ground turkey
1/2 onion, chopped
14-oz. can sauerkraut, drained

4 c. instant mashed potatoes, cooked
2 c. shredded Swiss cheese

Brown beef, turkey and onion together in a large skillet over medium heat. Place mixture into the bottom of an ungreased 13"x9" baking dish. Cover beef mixture with sauerkraut; top with mashed potatoes. Bake at 350 degrees for 30 to 35 minutes or until potatoes are golden brown. Top with cheese and bake an additional 5 minutes or until cheese is melted. Makes 4 to 6 servings.

If you can't make it better, you can laugh at it.

–Erma Bombeck

Southwestern Pork Chalupas

Vickie

*Try these instead of ground beef nachos...
family & friends will say Olé!*

2 15-oz. cans pinto beans,
   drained and rinsed
4 c. water
4-oz. can chopped green chiles
2 T. chili powder
2 t. ground cumin
1 t. dried oregano

salt and pepper to taste
4-lb. pork shoulder roast
16-oz. pkg. tortilla chips
Garnish: shredded Mexican-
   blend cheese, sour cream,
   salsa, sliced black olives,
   sliced jalapeño peppers

Combine beans, water, chiles and spices in a large slow cooker; mix well. Add roast; cover and cook on low setting for 4 hours. Remove roast and shred, discarding any bones; return pork to slow cooker. Cover and cook on low setting for an additional 2 to 4 hours, adding more water if necessary. To serve, arrange tortilla chips on serving plates. Spoon pork mixture over chips; garnish as desired. Makes 8 to 10 servings.

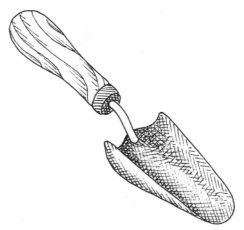

A good way to reheat rice without overcooking it is to steam it in a colander or sieve over a pot of boiling water, without letting the rice touch the water.

Tangy Citrus Chicken

Jo Ann

The lemonade adds a really refreshing taste to this dish.

8 boneless, skinless chicken
   breasts
6-oz. can frozen lemonade,
   thawed
3/4 c. molasses

1 t. dried savory
1/2 t. ground mustard
1/2 t. dried thyme
1/2 t. lemon juice

Place chicken in a 13"x9" baking dish coated with non-stick vegetable spray. In a medium mixing bowl, combine remaining ingredients; mix well. Pour half of the mixture over the chicken. Bake, uncovered, at 350 degrees for 20 minutes. Turn chicken; add remaining sauce. Bake an additional 15 to 20 minutes or until juices run clear. Makes 8 servings.

Rub soap on itchy mosquito bites...instant relief!

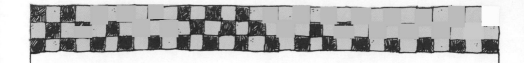

Filet Mignon with Mushrooms

Teresa Beal
Bowling Green, KY

A terrific choice for a special meal.

4 6-oz. filet mignon steaks
1/2 t. salt
1/2 t. pepper
1/2 t. garlic powder

12-oz. pkg. sliced mushrooms
4 cloves garlic, chopped
1/4 c. plus 2 T. Marsala wine

Sprinkle each steak with salt, pepper and garlic powder; set aside. Coat a large skillet with non-stick vegetable spray and heat to medium-high. Add mushrooms and garlic; cook, stirring frequently for 5 minutes or until mushrooms are golden. Remove from heat and set aside. Arrange steaks on a broiler pan about 4 inches below the heat source. Broil for about 4 minutes on each side or to desired doneness. In skillet, reheat mushroom mixture over medium-high heat. Add wine to mixture and bring to a boil; cook for about 2 minutes or until wine is reduced. Place each steak on a serving plate and top with mushroom mixture. Makes 4 servings.

Spray your plastic storage containers with non-stick vegetable spray before pouring tomato-based sauces in...no stains!

simple
Soups & Salads

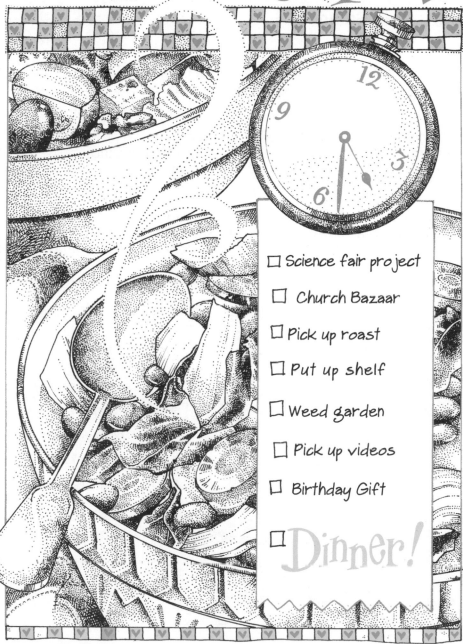

- ☐ Science fair project
- ☐ Church Bazaar
- ☐ Pick up roast
- ☐ Put up shelf
- ☐ Weed garden
- ☐ Pick up videos
- ☐ Birthday Gift

- ☐ Dinner!

"Counting time is not nearly as important as making time count."
— Unknown

Corn Chip Salad

Jayne Lammers
Quincy, IL

Hint...don't let this salad sit for too long, or the
corn chips will get mushy.

1 head lettuce, torn
2 c. shredded Cheddar cheese
1 onion, finely chopped

10-1/2 oz. pkg. corn chips,
   broken
12-oz. jar chili sauce
3/4 c. oil

In a large serving bowl, combine lettuce, cheese, onion and corn chips.
In a small mixing bowl, combine chili sauce and oil. Toss chili sauce
mixture over lettuce mixture until coated. Makes 4 to 6 servings.

To keep vegetables
fresh and nutritious,
wrap them in paper
towels and store
them in unsealed
plastic bags in
the refrigerator.

Simple Soups & Salads

Easy Potato Salad

Sharon Tillman
Hampton, VA

This is the first non-dessert recipe that my mother taught me to make.

1-oz. pkg. dry ranch salad
   dressing mix
1/2 c. mayonnaise
1/4 c. water

8 potatoes, cooked and cubed
1-1/2 c. celery, sliced
3/4 c. red onion, chopped

In a large serving bowl, combine dressing mix, mayonnaise and water. Add potatoes, celery and onion; toss to coat. Cover and refrigerate until ready to serve. Makes 4 to 6 servings.

Oriental Salad

Winnie Collins
Gurnee, IL

A well-loved summertime favorite.

1/4 c. olive oil
2 T. sugar
1 to 2 T. vinegar
2 t. soy sauce
3-oz. pkg. chicken ramen
   noodles with seasoning
   packet, divided

1 head lettuce, torn
1 head romaine lettuce, torn
1/2 c. slivered almonds

In a medium mixing bowl, combine olive oil, sugar, vinegar, soy sauce and ramen noodle seasoning packet together until sugar is dissolved. Break ramen noodles into small pieces. In a large serving bowl, combine ramen noodles, lettuce and almonds. Toss olive oil mixture with lettuce mixture to coat; let stand for 30 minutes for flavors to blend. Makes 8 to 10 servings.

Beef Stew

Laura Strausberger
Roswell, GA

This is a great make-ahead meal for a busy day.

2 lbs. stew beef
5 potatoes, chopped
14-1/2 oz. can diced tomatoes,
    undrained
7-3/4 oz. can pearl onions,
    drained

4 carrots, chopped
3 T. instant tapioca pudding mix
3 t. sugar
1 c. water
3/4 T. salt
pepper to taste

Combine all ingredients in a 6-quart slow cooker. Let simmer on high 4 to 5 hours. Makes 6 to 8 servings.

Quick Cabbage Soup

Yvonne Cifani
Oxford, MI

Top with Parmesan cheese and a slice of French bread.

1 lb. ground sirloin
2 T. oil
2 16-oz. cans stewed tomatoes
10-1/2 oz. can beef broth
2 c. water

1 t. lemon juice
1 t. Worcestershire sauce
1 head cabbage, chopped
salt and pepper to taste

In a large skillet, brown sirloin in oil; drain. In a large stockpot, place sirloin, tomatoes, broth, water, lemon juice and Worcestershire sauce; bring to a boil and simmer for 30 minutes. Place cabbage in stockpot and simmer for one hour; salt and pepper to taste. Makes 6 to 8 servings.

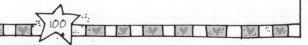

Texas Taco Soup

Denise Bennett
Anderson, IN

A neighbor who moved here from Texas shared this very hearty soup recipe. It's a nice alternative to chili...even our picky seven-year-old son loves it! Tomato juice can be added if you like a thinner consistency. This tastes even better the next day, if there's any left!

1 lb. ground beef
1/2 onion, diced
19-oz. can mild or hot chili
   beans
14-1/2 oz. can diced tomatoes
   with green chiles
1-oz. pkg. spicy ranch salad
   dressing mix

14-oz. can black beans, drained
14-3/4 oz. can shoepeg corn,
   drained
Garnish: tortilla strips, sour
   cream, shredded Cheddar
   cheese, diced green onions,
   sliced avocado

In a stockpot over medium heat, brown beef with onion; drain. Stir in undrained chili beans and tomatoes; add remaining ingredients. Reduce heat to low; cover and simmer for 30 minutes. Ladle into bowls and garnish as desired. Serves 6 to 8.

Line shelves with vintage handkerchiefs for
a touch of nostalgia.

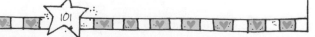

Simple Beef & Tortellini Soup

Cindy Neel
Gooseberry Patch

Serve with garlic bread for a quick and filling meal!

5 c. canned beef and beans
2 14-1/2 oz. cans beef broth
2 c. frozen mixed vegetables
1 c. frozen cheese tortellini

1 t. dried Italian seasoning
Garnish: grated Parmesan
   cheese

In a large stockpot, combine beef and beans, broth, vegetables, tortellini and Italian seasoning; bring to a boil. Reduce heat to medium; cook over medium heat for 8 to 10 minutes or until vegetables and tortellini are tender, stirring occasionally. Garnish with cheese. Makes 4 to 6 servings.

I buried a lot of my ironing in the backyard.

-Phyllis Diller

Southwestern Layered Salad

Tonya Sheppard
Galveston, TX

Served individually in one-pint Mason jars, this salad is great for taking on the road!

8-oz. container sour cream
3-oz. pkg. cream cheese,
   softened
10-oz. can tomatoes with green
   chiles, drained
1 t. cumin
4 c. romaine lettuce, shredded
2 to 3 tomatoes, chopped
15-oz. can black beans, drained
   and rinsed

15-oz. can corn, drained
1 sweet red onion, chopped
15-oz. can pinto beans, drained
   and rinsed
2 red peppers, chopped
Garnish: shredded sharp
   Cheddar cheese, green onion,
   chopped

Combine sour cream, cream cheese, tomatoes with chiles and cumin in a blender; process until smooth. Chill. Layer vegetables in order given among eight, one pint Mason jars. Spoon sour cream mixture over top; sprinkle with cheese and green onion. Cover and chill for one hour. Makes 8 servings.

Minimize shrinkage in bacon by running slices under lukewarm water before frying.

Maple Salad

Roxanne Bixby
West Franklin, NH

A great salad to share at your next church social.

8-oz. pkg. cream cheese,
   softened
1 c. maple syrup
20-oz. can crushed pineapple,
   drained

1 c. chopped dates
1 c. chopped walnuts
8 oz. whipped topping

In a large serving bowl, mix all ingredients together; chill until ready to serve. Makes 6 servings.

If you soak canned pineapple in cold water for half an hour,
it will taste more like fresh!

Panzanella Salad ▶

Denise Herr
Galloway, OH

I've made this several times. It's a beautiful summer presentation salad and SO delicious. Garden veggies are best but absolutely not necessary!

1/2 loaf Italian or French bread, cubed
1/4 c. olive oil
salt and pepper to taste
1 red pepper, chopped
1 yellow pepper, chopped
1 orange pepper, chopped
1 cucumber, chopped

1 red onion, chopped
1 pt. cherry or grape tomatoes
1 to 2 T. capers
6 leaves fresh basil, cut into long, thin strips
3/4 c. vinaigrette or Italian salad dressing

In a bowl, toss together bread, olive oil, salt and pepper. Spread on an ungreased baking sheet and bake at 350 degrees for 5 minutes, or until golden and crisp; let cool. In a bowl, combine remaining ingredients. Just before serving, add bread cubes and toss to coat. Makes 6 to 8 servings.

Warm Bacon Salad

Elaine Conway
Buffalo, NY

Toss together and enjoy.

1 head lettuce, torn
1/4 to 1/2 c. vinegar

4 slices bacon, crisply cooked and diced
salt and pepper to taste

Place lettuce in a large serving bowl. In a large saucepan, heat vinegar and bacon until boiling; add lettuce and toss to coat. Transfer back to serving bowl. Sprinkle with salt and pepper to taste. Makes 6 to 8 servings.

Sausage-Bean Chowder

Nancy Hines
Flushing, MI

The perfect meal for a cozy weekend at home.

1 lb. ground sausage
1 onion, chopped
16-oz. can chopped tomatoes,
   undrained

32-oz. jar Great Northern beans,
   rinsed and drained
1 potato, chopped
1/2 t. dried basil
2 c. water

In a large skillet, brown sausage and onion together. Place sausage and onion in a 4-quart slow cooker and add remaining ingredients; stir. Cook on low for 5 to 6 hours. Makes 6 servings.

Add a tangy twist to bean soup by drizzling some balsamic vinegar in while it simmers.

Chicken & Pasta Soup

John Sgambellone
Delaware, OH

Double this recipe and freeze half for another day.

2-1/2 lbs. chicken, cubed
1 qt. plus 14-oz. can chicken
   broth
16-oz. can green beans, drained

6-oz. can tomato paste
1 c. small shell macaroni,
   uncooked
1 t. dried basil

In a large stockpot, over medium-high heat, bring chicken and broth to a boil. Reduce heat, cover and simmer for 25 minutes or until chicken is tender. Remove chicken, cool slightly. Add remaining ingredients to broth. Heat to a boil, reduce heat. Cover and simmer for 20 minutes or until macaroni is tender. Add chicken back to soup and cook an additional 10 to 15 minutes. Makes 6 to 8 servings.

Homemade croutons absorb dressing much better than store-bought. Make your own easily by cubing bread and sprinkling them with Italian seasoning and olive oil. Toast on a baking sheet at 350 degrees until crisp.

Beer-Cheese Soup ▶

Holly Smith
Shaker Heights, OH

This is a favorite at our house during football season. Make it for lunch on a chilly autumn day...it will really warm you to your toes! It's just as tasty the next day too, if not tastier.

3 T. butter
1 onion, finely chopped
1 carrot, peeled and finely chopped
1 stalk celery, finely chopped
Optional: 1 jalapeño pepper, seeded and chopped
3 T. all-purpose flour
1 c. chicken broth
2 c. milk or half-and-half

2 c. shredded extra-sharp Cheddar cheese
1/2 c. beer or non-alcoholic beer, at room temperature
1/8 t. cayenne pepper
1/4 t. salt
1/4 t. pepper
Garnish: 2 T. green onions, chopped

Melt butter in a large saucepan over medium heat. Add onion, carrot, celery and jalapeño, if using; sauté until vegetables are crisp-tender. Add flour to vegetable mixture; stir well. In a small saucepan over medium heat, combine broth and milk or half-and-half; heat through. Pour broth mixture into vegetable mixture. Reduce heat to low and simmer, stirring occasionally, until soup begins to thicken, about 4 to 5 minutes. Stir in cheese and beer until cheese is completely melted. Stir in spices. Garnish with chopped green onions. Makes 4 servings.

Beer-Cheese Soup is traditionally topped with popcorn. Make it extra-cheesy and top a bowl with some cheesy popcorn...yum!

Seashell Macaroni Salad

Ann Sheppard
West Monroe, LA

This can be served warm or chilled...either way, it's great.!

12-oz. pkg. small shell
   macaroni, cooked
1/2 c. onion, chopped
1-1/2 c. mayonnaise

12-oz. can tuna, drained
1/2 c. green pepper, chopped
15-oz. can peas, drained
salt and pepper to taste

In a large serving bowl, combine macaroni and onion; chill. When cool, add mayonnaise, tuna, green pepper and peas. Salt and pepper to taste. Makes 6 servings.

Toasting nuts and spices intensifies their flavor. Add nuts to salads and use spices as a low-fat flavoring for stir-fries, soups and stews.

Redskin Potato Salad

Ellen Wyman
Toledo, OH

This is the quickest (and tastiest) potato salad ever!

8 to 10 redskin potatoes, cooked
    and chopped
2 to 3 green onions, chopped

1 to 2 c. ranch salad dressing
salt and pepper to taste

Combine potatoes and onions in a large serving bowl. Stir in ranch dressing; season with salt and pepper. Makes 6 to 8 servings.

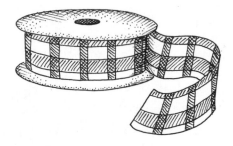

Sweet Potato Salad

Gloria Robertson
Midland, TX

*Sweet potatoes make this a nice change from
traditional potato salad.*

3 sweet potatoes, boiled and
    mashed
salt and pepper to taste
1/4 c. green onion, chopped

1/4 c. sugar
1/4 c. vinegar
1 egg, hard-boiled and sliced

In a large serving bowl, combine potatoes, salt, pepper, onion, sugar and vinegar. Top with egg slices. Chill before serving. Makes 4 servings.

Roasted Walnut & Pear Salad

Laurie Johnson
Rosenberg, TX

This is wonderful for a formal dinner or a casual, warm family gathering. Be sure to use fresh pears for the best flavor.

1 head romaine lettuce, torn
2 c. pears, thinly sliced
2 Roma tomatoes, chopped
1 c. walnuts
2 T. butter

1/4 c. brown sugar, packed
4-oz. pkg. crumbled blue cheese
8-oz. bottle raspberry white
    wine vinegar salad dressing

Place lettuce in a large serving bowl; lay pears on top and add tomatoes. In a medium skillet, roast walnuts in butter until golden; add brown sugar and stir over low heat until walnuts are hardened with glaze. Add walnuts to salads, sprinkle on blue cheese and toss with vinegar dressing. Makes 6 to 8 servings.

Place unripened pears in a plastic zipping bag with ripe bananas...the pears will ripen in no time.

Smoked Sausage Stew

Annette Ingram
Grand Rapids, MI

My husband can hardly wait for this soup each winter.

1-1/4 lbs. smoked sausage,
   sliced
16-oz. can onion soup
16-oz. can whole tomatoes,
   undrained

2 c. potatoes, cubed
1/2 t. Worcestershire sauce
15-1/4 oz. can corn, drained and
   1/2 c. liquid reserved
1/4 c. all-purpose flour

In a Dutch oven, cook sausage until browned; drain. Add onion soup, tomatoes, potatoes, Worcestershire sauce and corn. Bring mixture to a boil. Reduce heat and simmer for 20 minutes or until potatoes are tender. Stir reserved corn liquid into flour; gradually add to sausage mixture. Cook over medium heat, stirring constantly, until thick. Makes 4 to 6 servings.

Is the soup or stew too salty? Just add a peeled, raw potato and simmer. The potato will absorb the excess salt.

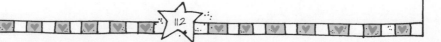

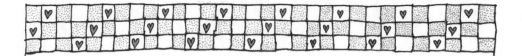

Nacho Soup

Ellen Downey
Versailles, KY

Quick, easy and very tasty.

10-oz. can tomatoes with chilies, undrained
10-3/4 oz. can vegetable beef soup
15-1/4 oz. corn, drained

15-oz. can chili with beans
10-3/4 oz. can tomato soup
Garnish: corn chips, sour cream or shredded Cheddar cheese

In a large stockpot, simmer all ingredients over medium-high heat until hot. In individual serving bowls, place a handful of corn chips, pour in soup and top with sour cream or cheese. Makes 6 servings.

Onion Soup

Penny Sherman
Cumming, GA

This is the best onion soup I've ever made...and I've tried a lot!

6 onions, halved and thickly sliced
2 T. bacon drippings
6 c. beef broth

6 T. dry sherry
4 to 6 slices French bread, toasted
4 to 6 slices Provolone cheese

Sauté onions in bacon drippings. Add beef broth and sherry; simmer for 15 minutes. Ladle into individual oven-proof bowls and top each with a slice of toast. Place cheese over bread and place bowls on a baking sheet. Bake at 350 degrees for 12 to 15 minutes or until the cheese is melted. Makes 4 to 6 servings.

Crunchy Apple-Pear Salad

Sharon Wilson
Palmyra, PA

Toss together green Granny Smith apples with red Anjou or Bartlett pears...so colorful!

2 apples, cored and cubed
2 pears, cored and thinly sliced
1 T. lemon juice
2 heads butter lettuce, torn into bite-size pieces
1/2 c. crumbled gorgonzola cheese

1 c. oil
6 T. cider vinegar
1/2 c. sugar
1 t. celery seed
1/2 t. salt
1/4 t. pepper
1/2 c. chopped walnuts, toasted

Toss apples and pears with lemon juice; drain. Arrange lettuce on 6 salad plates; top with apples, pears and cheese. Combine remaining ingredients except walnuts in a jar with a tight-fitting lid. Cover; shake well until dressing is blended and sugar dissolves. Drizzle salad with dressing; sprinkle with walnuts. Serve immediately. Serves 6.

Keep giftwrap handy for last-minute gifts. Store rolls of paper and plenty of ribbon in a pretty crock...charming in the corner of the craft room.

Old-Fashioned Potato Soup

Donna Zink
Lapeer, MI

There is nothing better than potato soup on a cold, blustery day...and this recipe's so quick!

8 potatoes, boiled and cubed
4-1/4 c. milk, divided
salt and pepper to taste

1 T. butter
1/2 c. all-purpose flour
1 egg, beaten

In a large stockpot, combine potatoes and 4 cups milk; season with salt and pepper. Heat mixture over medium-high heat for 15 to 20 minutes or until potatoes are tender. In a medium mixing bowl, blend butter and flour together; add egg and remaining milk. Drop by teaspoonfuls into potato mixture. Cover and cook an additional 10 minutes, stirring occasionally. Makes 4 servings.

Place an apple into your bag of potatoes to keep them from budding.

Yellow Squash Soup

Roxanne Bixby
West Franklin, NH

Serve this soup hot or cold. Substitute vanilla yogurt when
serving it cold for just the right flavor.

1 yellow squash, sliced   pepper to taste
1 onion, sliced   1/8 c. plain yogurt
14-1/2 oz. can chicken broth

In a medium stockpot, cook squash and onion in broth for 15 minutes
over medium-high heat. Add pepper and yogurt; purée in blender until
smooth. Return to saucepan and heat until warm. Makes 2 servings.

A smile is a curve that sets everything straight.

–Phyllis Diller

Hearty Kielbasa & Kale Soup

Kathy Royer
Charlotte, NC

This flavorful soup is rich and delicious.

8 oz. kielbasa, sliced	2 14-1/2 oz. cans chicken broth
1 lb. kale, chopped	15 oz. can Great Northern beans,
1 onion, chopped	rinsed and drained
1 potato, cubed	1 t. dried thyme
3 cloves garlic, minced	1 t. pepper

In a medium stockpot over medium heat, cook the first 5 ingredients for 5 minutes; stirring frequently until kale begins to wilt and sausage browns. Stir in the next 4 ingredients. Increase heat to high; bring to a boil. Reduce heat to medium; partially cover and simmer for 12 minutes or until potatoes are tender. Makes 6 to 8 servings.

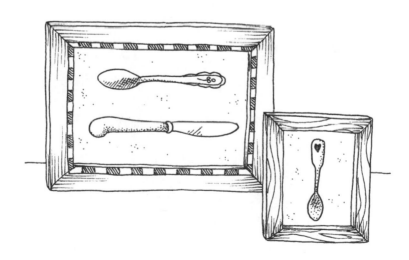

A sweet remembrance...place your child's first spoon or Grandma's old silver into a shadow box.

Taffy Apple Salad

Wendy Holloway
Gaylord, MI

This salad tastes exactly like caramel apples!

1/2 c. sugar
1 T. all-purpose flour
1 egg
2 T. apple cider vinegar
8-oz. can crushed pineapple,
   drained and juice reserved

4 to 6 c. red, yellow and green
   apples, cored and sliced
2-1/2 c. salted peanuts, divided
8 oz. whipped topping

In a medium saucepan, over low heat bring sugar, flour, egg, vinegar and pineapple juice to a boil, stirring constantly. Remove from heat and cool. Place apples into a large serving bowl; add pineapple and 2 cups peanuts. Fold in sugar mixture and whipped topping; top with remaining peanuts. Makes 10 servings.

Be creative with leftover dinner biscuits...spoon berries and whipped cream on them for a fresh dessert, or place a sausage patty and a cooked egg on one for breakfast.

Broccoli-Cauliflower Salad

Renee Johnson
Smithville, TN

Make this the night before the company potluck.

5 c. broccoli, chopped
2-1/2 c. cauliflower, chopped
1 onion, chopped
2 c. cherry tomatoes, halved

1 c. mayonnaise
1/2 c. sour cream
1 T. sugar
1 T. vinegar

In a large serving bowl, combine broccoli, cauliflower, onion and tomatoes. In a separate small mixing bowl, combine remaining ingredients until well blended. Toss dressing with broccoli mixture; chill at least 6 hours. Makes 6 to 8 servings.

Mozzarella & Tomato Salad

Zoe Bennett
Columbia, SC

A tasty salad for cheese lovers.

8 tomatoes, chopped
8 T. olive oil
pepper to taste

16-oz. pkg. shredded mozzarella cheese
10 sprigs fresh basil, torn

In a large serving bowl, combine all ingredients; toss to coat. Cover and refrigerate for 30 minutes before serving. Makes 8 servings.

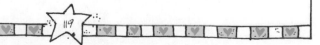

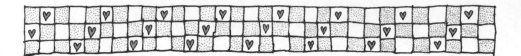

French Stew

Mary Gildenpfennig
Harsens Island, MI

This recipe was shared with me by my grandmother.

1 lb. bacon, chopped
1 onion, chopped
2 14-oz. cans chopped
    tomatoes, undrained

15-1/4 oz. can peas, drained
3 T. all-purpose flour
1 c. water

In a medium stockpot, over medium-high heat, cook bacon and onion together until onion is clear and bacon is crispy. Add tomatoes and peas; bring to a boil. Mash tomatoes and peas as they boil. Reduce to simmer. Mix flour and water together; slowly add to bacon mixture and heat until thickened. Makes 4 servings.

Tomatoes will stay fresh longer when placed stem down.

Tomatoes & Cucumber Salad

Ann Fehr
Trappe, PA

The honey gives it a hint of sweetness.

1 cucumber, diced
1 tomato, diced
2 T. onion, chopped

1 T. lemon juice
2 T. honey

In a medium serving bowl, mix all ingredients together; chill before serving. Makes 2 to 4 servings.

Frozen Apricot Salad

Pat Smith
Bonham, TX

A refreshing salad for those hot summer days.

2 12-oz. pkgs. frozen
   strawberries, thawed
12-oz. can apricot pie filling

16-1/2 oz. can pineapple tidbits,
   juice reserved
3 bananas, chopped
2/3 c. sugar

In a large serving bowl, stir all ingredients together until sugar is dissolved. Pour mixture into muffin tins. Place in freezer for at least 4 hours. Fifteen minutes prior to serving; remove from freezer. Makes 12 servings.

Chicken Noodle Soup for Two

Angie Lengacher
Montgomery, IN

An outstanding soup for a cozy evening.

2 c. water
2 cubes chicken bouillon
5-oz. can cooked chicken,
   undrained
2 T. onion, chopped
1 bay leaf

1/8 t. pepper
1/4 c. medium egg noodles,
   uncooked
1 T. celery, chopped
2 t. dried parsley

In a medium stockpot, bring water to a boil; add chicken bouillon and stir to dissolve. Add chicken, onion, bay leaf and pepper; bring to a boil. Cover and simmer for 8 to 10 minutes. Remove bay leaf. Add noodles, celery and parsley; simmer an additional 8 to 10 minutes or until noodles are tender. Makes 2 servings.

Spray ice cube trays with a bit of non-stick vegetable spray and the cubes will fall right out.

Festive Fruit Salad

Virginia Watson
Scranton, PA

This recipe is easily doubled for a family picnic.

1 red apple, cored and chopped
1 green apple, cored and
   chopped
2 plums, pitted and sliced

2 stalks celery, sliced
1/2 c. dried cranberries
1/2 c. chopped almonds
8-oz. carton lemon yogurt

In a large bowl, combine apples, plums, celery, cranberries and almonds. Stir in yogurt. Chill for at least one hour. Makes 6 servings.

Farmer's Wife Salad

Coli Harrington
Delaware, OH

The ingredients in this salad are almost always on hand at my house.

1 head broccoli, chopped
1 head romaine lettuce, torn
1 pt. cherry tomatoes, halved
1 c. mayonnaise-type salad
   dressing

3-1/2 T. sugar
1-1/4 T. vinegar
3/4 lb. bacon, crisply cooked
   and crumbled

In a large mixing bowl, combine broccoli, lettuce and tomatoes. In a separate medium mixing bowl, combine salad dressing, sugar and vinegar; pour over lettuce mixture and toss to coat. Sprinkle with bacon and chill before serving. Makes 8 servings.

Country Cole Slaw

Wendy Paffenroth
Pine Island, NY

This recipe is from the 1940's and it's fabulous!

3 c. shredded cabbage
1 c. carrot, shredded
1/2 c. whipping cream

3 T. apple cider vinegar
salt and pepper to taste

In a large mixing bowl, combine cabbage and carrot. In a separate small mixing bowl, whip the cream and vinegar slowly. Add salt and pepper; pour over the cabbage and toss to coat. Chill before serving. Makes 6 servings.

When nothing is sure, everything is possible.

-Margaret Drabble

Pepperoni-Pasta Salad

Nancy Wise
Little Rock, AR

Try different blends of vegetables to match the season.

16-oz. pkg. frozen mixed
  vegetables, thawed
2 c. elbow macaroni, cooked
2-1/2 oz. pkg. sliced pepperoni

1/2 c. peppercorn-ranch salad
  dressing
salt and pepper to taste

In a large serving bowl, combine vegetables, macaroni and pepperoni. Toss dressing over pasta mixture. Season with salt and pepper. Cover and chill before serving. Makes 4 servings.

Never cut your lettuce
or greens with a knife or
kitchen scissors. Always
hand-tear to keep your
greens from browning
on the edges.

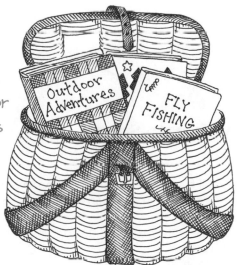

Clam Chowder

Pamela Line
Granite City, IL

Start this on a weekend morning and it's ready by lunchtime.

1 onion, chopped
1 stick butter
2 10-3/4 oz. cans clam chowder
3 10-3/4 oz. cans cream of
   potato soup

6-1/2 oz. can minced clams,
   drained
1 qt. half-and-half

In a small skillet, sauté onion in butter until tender. In a 6-quart slow cooker, combine with soups and clams. Cover and heat on low for 4 to 6 hours. Add half-and-half during last 2 hours of cooking. Makes 6 servings.

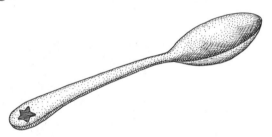

Zesty Tomato Soup

Jane Ramicone
Berea, OH

This is the easiest tomato soup...and everyone thinks I make it from scratch!

2 10-3/4 oz. cans tomato soup
2-2/3 c. water
2 t. chili powder

1 t. cayenne pepper
Garnish: oyster crackers and
   shredded provolone cheese

In a medium stockpot, combine all ingredients over medium-high heat; heat through. Pour into individual serving bowls and garnish with crackers and cheese. Makes 4 servings.

Baked Potato Soup

Robin Hill
Rochester, NY

Serve this soup with some favorite potato toppings...Cheddar
cheese, green onions and even salsa.

6 potatoes
1/3 c. butter
1/3 c. all-purpose flour

4 c. milk
1 c. sour cream

Pierce potatoes with a fork; microwave on high for 10 minutes, turn
and microwave an additional 10 minutes or until done. In a medium
stockpot, make a roux over low heat of butter and flour; mix together.
When thick, blend in milk. Continue cooking over medium heat for
5 to 10 minutes. Peel and cube potatoes; mashing half. Add potatoes
to milk mixture. Blend in sour cream; heat until warm. Makes 4 to
6 servings.

To keep your hands smelling sweet while cutting onions, try
rubbing your hands with the cut end of a stalk of celery.

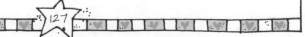

Hearty Winter Soup

Mary Tolliver
Welch, WV

Take a bowl of this soup and a cheerful flower to a friend feeling under the weather...a nice pick-me-up.

10-3/4 oz. can bean soup with bacon
10-3/4 oz. can cream of potato soup

14-1/2 oz. can stewed tomatoes, chopped and undrained
salt and pepper to taste
Garnish: shredded mozzarella cheese

In a medium stockpot, combine soups and tomatoes; salt and pepper to taste. Heat until boiling; let stand several minutes before serving. Top with cheese. Makes 4 to 6 servings.

Fast Corn Chowder

Janet Fuess
Ilion, NY

Simply scrumptious!

17-oz. can cream-style corn
12-oz. can evaporated milk
12-oz. can corn with sweet peppers, undrained

1 t. dried minced onion
1/8 t. pepper
1 T. butter

In a large stockpot, combine all ingredients, except butter; bring to a boil. Add butter and heat until melted. Makes 4 servings.

Old-Fashioned Blueberry Pancakes, page 76

Beer-Cheese Soup, page 108

Bubbly Cheese Garlic Bread, page 11

Crunchy Apple-Pear Salad, page 115

High Rollers, page 34

Mile-High Coconut Cream Pie, page 182

Panzanella Salad, page 105

Dried Beef Cheese Ball, page 32

Chicken & Barley Soup, page 132

Country Harvest Pie, page 183

Texas Taco Soup, page 101

Vickie's Tomato Pie, page 65

Triple-Take Grilled Cheese, page 31

Apricot-Glased Carrots, page 143

Southwestern Layered Salad, page 103

Family-Favorite
Mac & Cheese, page 158

Incredible Mini Burger Bites, page 29

Cheesy Beef & Bacon Meatloaf, page 63

Twice-Baked Potato Casserole, page 161

Southwestern Pork Chalupas, page 94

Pecan Pie Bars, page 184

Taffy Apple Cupcakes, page 185

Buckeye Brownies, page 174

Giant Cream Puffs, page 192

White Chicken Chili

Nancy Willis
Farmington Hills, MI

This flavorful recipe can turn leftover chicken or turkey into a savory soup.

2 lbs. cooked chicken, chopped
48-oz. jar Great Northern beans,
   rinsed and drained
16-oz. jar salsa

8-oz. pkg. shredded Monterey
   Jack with jalapeño cheese
2 t. cumin
1/2 c. water

Combine all ingredients in a large stockpot; cover and simmer for one hour, stirring occasionally. Add water as needed. Makes 4 to 6 servings.

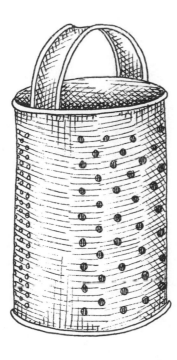

A quick & easy
way to crush
tomatoes is to cut
them in half, and with the
cut side down, rub against
a grater. In no time
just the peel is left in
your hand.

Sweet Pea & Noodle Salad

Kerry Mayer
Dunham Springs, LA

Use alphabet pasta for a fun meal for your kids.

12-oz. pkg. spiral pasta, cooked
10-oz. pkg. frozen peas
1 onion, chopped

1/2 c. mayonnaise-type salad
    dressing
1/4 t. hot pepper sauce

In a large serving bowl, combine pasta, peas, onion, salad dressing and hot pepper sauce. Mix well and chill before serving. Makes 8 servings.

Add fresh herbs such as basil, oregano or chives to your next summer salad.

Creamy Orange Salad

Melody Taynor
Everett, WA

My family gets so excited when I tell them we're having "creamy salad."

6-oz. pkg. orange gelatin mix
1 c. boiling water
3-oz. pkg. cream cheese
1/2 c. mayonnaise

1 T. vinegar
1-1/2 c. carrot, grated
8-oz. can pineapple tidbits,
    drained

In a medium serving bowl, combine gelatin and water; stir until dissolved. Add cream cheese, mayonnaise and vinegar; mix until blended and refrigerate until partially set. Add carrot and pineapple; mix well and chill until set. Makes 6 servings.

Pineapple Salad

Beth Goblirsch
Minneapolis, MN

This is my mother's recipe. My dad and I enjoyed as much of it as we wanted, since no one else liked coconut.

1 c. sour cream
1 c. canned pineapple chunks
1 c. canned mandarin oranges

1 c. mini marshmallows
1 c. flaked coconut

In a large serving bowl, mix all ingredients together. Refrigerate at least 4 hours before serving to blend flavors. Makes 8 servings.

Chicken & Barley Soup

Angela Murphy
Tempe, AZ

We like to substitute leftover turkey from Thanksgiving dinner in this hearty, quick & easy soup. It's a terrific pick-me-up after a day of post-Thanksgiving shopping.

1 c. onion, chopped
1 c. carrot, peeled and chopped
1/2 c. celery, chopped
2 cloves garlic, minced
2 t. olive oil
2 14-1/2 oz. cans chicken broth

1/2 c. quick-cooking barley, uncooked
1-3/4 c. water
1/4 t. salt
1/4 t. pepper
1 c. cooked chicken, cubed

In a Dutch oven over medium-high heat, sauté onion, carrot, celery and garlic in oil for 5 minutes, until onion is tender. Add broth, barley, water and seasonings. Bring to a boil; reduce heat and simmer, partially covered, about 25 minutes, until vegetables are tender. Add chicken; heat through. Serves 4.

Place packets of seeds in a basket by your front door...let visitors pick their favorite pack to take home. As the flowers bloom, friends will be reminded of you.

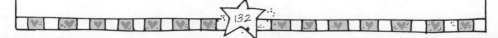

Mexican Potato Soup

Kim Scherler
Walters, OK

Hits the spot on a chilly evening.

2 10-3/4 oz. cans potato soup
2 c. milk
4 oz. shredded Monterey Jack
   with jalapeño cheese
15-oz. can plus 7-oz. can corn,
   drained

1/4 c. pimento cheese spread
6 slices bacon, crisply cooked
   and crumbled
1 t. onion powder
salt and pepper to taste

In a large saucepan, mix together all ingredients over medium heat, stirring often, for 15 to 20 minutes or until hot and cheese is melted. Makes 6 servings.

Noodles & Ground Beef Soup

Sue Utley
Papillion, NE

One of our favorite soups...old-fashioned and delicious!

1 lb. ground beef, browned
1 qt. water
1 onion, chopped
1 stalk celery, chopped
salt and pepper to taste

2 T. beef bouillon granules
2 T. dried parsley
1 qt. tomato juice
12-oz. pkg. wide egg noodles,
   uncooked

In a large saucepan, crumble ground beef into water. Add onion, celery, salt and pepper. Boil slowly until vegetables are tender. Add bouillon and parsley. Add juice and noodles; cook for 10 minutes or until noodles are tender. Makes 8 servings.

Peas & Pasta Salad

Hollie Halverson
Merrimack, NH

Add onions and hot peppers for a zippier flavor.

2 c. wagon wheel pasta,
   uncooked
2 carrots, thinly sliced
1 c. frozen peas
1/4 c. mayonnaise

1/4 c. plain yogurt
1 t. sugar
1/2 t. salt
1/8 t. pepper

Cook pasta according to package directions; add carrots in the last 7 minutes of cooking and drain. Stir in peas, rinse with cold water to chill. Drain again and transfer to a large serving bowl. In a medium mixing bowl, stir together the mayonnaise, yogurt, sugar, salt and pepper. Pour dressing over pasta and vegetables; toss to coat. Makes 6 servings.

Mexican Cucumber Salad

Wendy Campbell
Ostrander, OH

A tasty springtime salad.

2-1/2 c. cucumbers, diced
2 c. diced tomatoes, drained
1/4 c. Vidalia onion, minced
8 oz. sour cream

3/4 t. dried cilantro
3/4 t. cumin
1/2 t. garlic powder
1/2 t. salt

In a large serving bowl, combine cucumbers, tomatoes and onion. In a medium mixing bowl, combine remaining ingredients; toss with cucumber mixture. Makes 4 to 6 servings.

Speedy Sides

- ☐ Wash windows
- ☐ Return library books
- ☐ Clean closet
- ☐ Choir practice
- ☐ Lunch with Jo Ann
- ☐ Repot plants
- ☐ Ironing
- ☐ Dinner!

"There is nothing wrong with the world that a sensible woman could not settle in an afternoon." -Jean Giraudoux

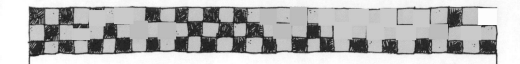

Granny's Slow Cooker Taters

Ruth Payne Palmer
Glendale, UT

I can place all the ingredients into the slow cooker in record time and forget about it as I go about the tasks of a busy day.

32-oz. pkg. frozen hash browns
1 lb. kielbasa, chopped
1 onion, diced

10-3/4 oz. can cheese soup
1 soup can milk

Place all ingredients into a 6-quart slow cooker; stir to mix. Cover and cook on high for 3 hours or on low for 8 to 10 hours. Makes 6 servings.

Use a slow cooker for dishes that you would normally cook on the stove. Try stews, chili or even chicken and noodles. It cooks by itself so you have a little more time with family & friends.

Speedy Sides

Creamed Tomatoes

Regina Vining
Warwick, RI

My mom used to make this for my brothers and I when we were feeling under the weather.

4 tomatoes, sliced
1 T. all-purpose flour
1 c. milk

1/2 t. salt
12-oz. tube refrigerated biscuits, baked

Place tomatoes into a large saucepan; bring to a boil. In a small mixing bowl, combine flour with milk to make a thin liquid mixture. Blend flour mixture into tomatoes; add salt, stirring occasionally. Return to a boil. Serve over biscuits. Makes 4 to 6 servings.

Jane's Potatoes

Karen Slack
Mount Pleasant, TX

I got this recipe from a dear friend over 30 years ago. We have so many happy memories.

32-oz. pkg. frozen hash browns
1 onion, chopped
10-3/4 oz. can cream of potato soup
10-3/4 oz. can cream of mushroom soup

16 oz. sour cream
2 t. seasoned salt
1 sleeve saltine crackers, crushed
1 stick butter, melted

In a large mixing bowl, combine hash browns, onion, soups, sour cream and salt together. Pour into a lightly greased 13"x9" baking dish. Top with crackers and pour butter over all. Bake, uncovered, at 350 degrees for one hour. Makes 18 servings.

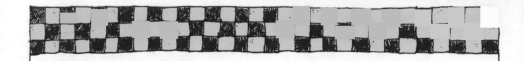

Delicious Corn Pudding

Robyn Wright
Delaware, OH

This is the easiest recipe... just combine and cook!

2 16-oz. cans cream-style corn
4 eggs, beaten
4 T. all-purpose flour
1/4 c. butter, melted

1 c. milk
1/2 c. sugar
1/2 t. salt

Combine all ingredients in a large mixing bowl. Pour into a lightly greased 2-quart baking dish. Bake, uncovered, at 350 degrees for 1-1/4 to 1-1/2 hours. Makes 8 to 10 servings.

Make herb butter for corn on the cob by mixing butter in a food processor with fresh, chopped dill, thyme or basil.

Rice Pilaf with Almonds

Susan Young
Madison, AL

Garnish with a sprig of fresh parsley...a classic finishing touch.

3/4 c. onion, diced
1/2 c. slivered almonds
1 T. butter

2 c. chicken broth
2 c. instant white rice, uncooked

In a large saucepan, sauté onion and almonds in butter until slightly browned. Add broth and rice; bring to a boil. Remove from heat and cover pan. Let stand for 10 minutes, stirring occasionally. Makes 4 servings.

When carving a pumpkin, rub the edges with petroleum jelly to keep them from withering.

Honey-Dill Carrots

Sandy Smith
Tolland, CT

A great way to encourage the kids to eat carrots.

4 carrots, sliced
1-1/2 T. honey

1/4 to 1/2 t. dried dill weed

In a medium saucepan, cook carrots, covered, in about 2 inches of water for 10 to 12 minutes, or until tender, but not mushy. Add honey and dill; stir until coated. Makes 4 servings.

Scalloped Onions

Mary Maxwell
Parsons, KS

This is an easy 3-ingredient recipe that's yummy served with meat loaf, a roastor even a simple hamburger meal.

6 onions, sliced
3 c. potato chips, crushed

8-oz. pkg. pasteurized process
cheese spread, cubed

In a large saucepan, boil onions until clear. Layer half of the onions alternately with half of the potato chips and cheese in a greased 2-quart baking dish; repeat layers ending with cheese. Bake, uncovered, at 350 degrees for 20 to 25 minutes. Makes 4 servings.

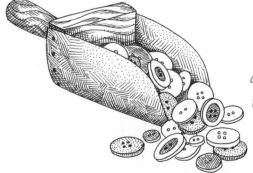

Fill canning jars with colorful charms, penny candy, marbles or even mini cookie cutters...so charming.

Speedy Sides

Cheesy Cauliflower

John Alexander
New Britain, CT

Use spicy brown mustard for a bold flavor!

1-1/4 t. mayonnaise
1-1/4 t. mustard
1 head cauliflower, chopped and
   cooked

1/4 c. butter, sliced
3/4 c. grated Parmesan cheese

In a small mixing bowl, combine mayonnaise and mustard. Place cauliflower in an ungreased 2-quart baking dish; spread with mustard mixture and dot with butter. Sprinkle with cheese. Bake, uncovered, at 375 degrees for 30 minutes. Makes 4 to 6 servings.

Red Cabbage

Rita Morgan
Pueblo, CO

My mother used to make this for us when we were little...it's still one of my favorites.

1 onion, diced
3 slices bacon, crisply cooked,
   crumbled and drippings
   reserved
1 head red cabbage, shredded

1 red apple, cored and cubed
1 t. vinegar
1 t. sugar
salt to taste

In a large skillet, sauté onion in bacon drippings; add cabbage, apple and bacon. Place cabbage mixture in a large saucepan; cover with water. Cook over medium-high heat until tender, drain and season with vinegar and sugar. Add salt to taste. Makes 8 servings.

Easy Skillet Eggplant

Pamela Tucker
Jet, OK

A tasty way to introduce your family to eggplant.

1 eggplant, cubed
1 zucchini, sliced
1 green pepper, sliced

1 red onion, sliced
3 T. French salad dressing
2 c. cherry tomatoes

Place all ingredients, except tomatoes, in a large skillet. Cover and cook over low heat for 10 minutes, or until tender. Add tomatoes and cook an additional 3 to 5 minutes; serve hot. Makes 4 servings.

Spinach Soufflé

Gloria Robertson
Midland, TX

If you'd like, use Swiss cheese instead of Cheddar.

10-oz. pkg. frozen, chopped
   spinach, thawed
3 T. all-purpose flour
3 eggs, beaten

1/2 t. salt
12-oz. carton cottage cheese
4 oz. shredded Cheddar cheese
1/4 c. butter, melted

In a large mixing bowl, combine spinach with flour; add eggs, salt, cottage cheese, Cheddar cheese and butter. Place in a greased 13"x9" baking dish. Bake, covered, at 375 degrees for 45 minutes. Uncover and bake an additional 15 minutes. Makes 6 servings.

Apricot-Glazed Carrots

Jill Burton
Gooseberry Patch

This is the only way my son Andy will eat cooked carrots!

6 c. carrots, peeled and sliced
3 T. butter, melted
1/3 c. apricot preserves
1/4 t. nutmeg

1/4 t. salt
2 t. lemon juice
Optional: 1 t. orange zest
Garnish: chopped fresh parsley

Place carrots in a large saucepan; cover with water. Bring to a boil and simmer until tender, 8 to 10 minutes; drain. In a bowl, combine remaining ingredients except parsley. Add carrots and stir to coat. Sprinkle with parsley. Serves 4 to 6.

If you get a splinter, place a piece of tape over it, then gently peel away. It'll remove the splinter painlessly and easily.

Broccoli Bake

Laura Strausberger
Roswell, GA

A speedy side to make when you have unexpected company.

3 eggs
1 c. all-purpose flour
1 c. milk
1 onion, chopped

3/4 lb. shredded Cheddar cheese
10-oz. pkg. frozen, chopped
   broccoli, thawed
1 t. baking powder

In a large mixing bowl, combine all ingredients. Place in a greased 13"x9" baking dish. Bake, uncovered, at 350 degrees for 35 minutes. Makes 2 to 4 servings.

Freeze water-filled balloons to keep handy for the kids' bumps and bruises. Wrap in a towel before using. Feels great and it's more fun than a regular ice pack.

Baked Zucchini Gratin

Heather Anne Kehr
Littlestown, PA

Double the recipe for a terrific potluck dish!

1 onion, sliced
2 lbs. zucchini, sliced
1 stick butter, melted and
   divided

2 c. shredded mozzarella cheese
1/2 c. bread crumbs
1/4 c. grated Parmesan cheese

In a lightly greased 2-quart baking dish, layer onion and zucchini. Drizzle with 1/4 cup butter; sprinkle with mozzarella cheese. In a separate bowl, combine remaining butter, bread crumbs and Parmesan cheese. Sprinkle crumb mixture evenly over the top. Bake, uncovered, at 350 degrees for 35 to 40 minutes or until zucchini is tender. Makes 8 servings.

Making baked potatoes? Thread the potatoes onto metal skewers before baking. The metal will speed up the cooking time.

Sweet Potato Chips

Lisa Donnelly
Oak Lawn, IL

Spicy and oh, so tasty!

1 t. sugar
1 t. salt
1-1/2 T. chili powder

1/4 to 1/2 t. cumin
2 sweet potatoes, thinly sliced

Combine sugar, salt, chili powder and cumin in a small mixing bowl; set aside. Place potato slices on a lightly greased baking sheet. Sprinkle lightly with half of sugar mixture. Bake at 325 degrees for 15 minutes; turn slices over and sprinkle with remaining sugar mixture. Bake an additional 15 minutes. Remove from oven and place on wire rack to cool. Makes 4 servings.

The future belongs to those who believe in
the beauty of their dreams.

-Eleanor Roosevelt

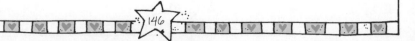

Speedy Sides

Mom's Scalloped Pineapple

Amy Heitsenrether
Clearfield, PA

Serve as a side dish or add a scoop of vanilla ice cream for a wonderful dessert.

1 stick butter, sliced
4 c. soft bread crumbs
2 c. sugar
3 eggs

1/2 c. evaporated milk
16-oz. can crushed pineapple,
    undrained
Garnish: cinnamon

In a medium mixing bowl, combine all ingredients and place in an ungreased 13"x9" baking dish. Bake, uncovered, at 350 degrees for 45 to 55 minutes. Sprinkle with cinnamon before serving. Makes 12 servings.

Cranberry Relish

Sandy Kelley
West Salem, WI

It sounds strange, but leave the orange peel on...it adds a great flavor!

1 red apple, cored and halved
2 seedless oranges, halved
12-oz. pkg. cranberries

1 c. sugar
3-oz. pkg. cranberry gelatin mix
1/2 c. chopped walnuts

Place fruit in a food processor; grind. Add remaining ingredients and mix again. Chill before serving. Makes 8 to 10 servings.

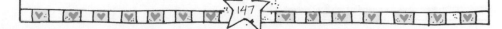

Baked Stuffed Tomatoes

Gail Prather
Bethel, MN

*I grow lots of tomatoes and herbs in my garden each year.
This recipe is one of our favorite side dishes that
uses the garden's bounty.*

6 tomatoes, cored, pulp removed
   and reserved
2 T. butter, melted
1 T. dried chives
1/2 t. dried parsley

1/4 t. dried thyme
1/4 t. dried sage
2 c. bread crumbs
1/2 c. finely shredded Cheddar
   cheese

In a medium mixing bowl, combine tomato pulp, butter, chives,
parsley, thyme, sage and bread crumbs together. Spoon filling into
tomato shells. Place tomatoes in an ungreased 13"x9" baking dish;
sprinkle with cheese. Bake, uncovered, at 350 degrees for 20 to
30 minutes. Makes 6 servings.

*Keep tomatoes out of the fridge for
fresh-from-the-garden taste.*

Brown Sugar Baked Beans

Debbie Cottrell
Petersburg, VA

The easiest baked beans ever!

2 15-oz. cans pork and beans
1 onion, chopped

1 c. catsup
1/4 c. brown sugar, packed

Mix all ingredients together in a ungreased 13"x9" baking dish. Bake, uncovered, at 350 degrees for 30 minutes. Makes 6 to 8 servings.

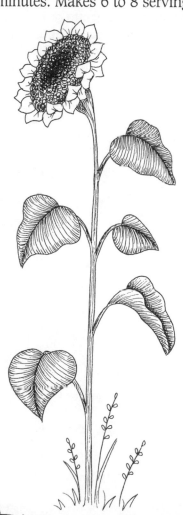

Create a cheerful, harvest table runner. Lay sunflower blooms down the center of the table. Place candles and small, brightly colored gourds and pumpkins around them.

Sweet Onion Casserole

Karen Cary
Marshalltown, IA

I make this dish year 'round.

5 sweet onions, sliced
1 stick butter
16-oz. pkg. shredded Cheddar
   cheese

2 c. round, buttery crackers,
   crushed

In a medium skillet, sauté onions in butter until clear. Place 1/2 of onions in an ungreased 2-quart baking dish; spread half of cheese over onions. Sprinkle 1/2 of crackers over all; repeat. Bake, uncovered, at 350 degrees for 30 minutes. Makes 8 servings.

Place just a corner of a bread slice between your teeth while you're cutting onions and your eyes won't water.

Speedy Sides

Roasted Parmesan Red Potatoes

Susan Young
Madison, AL

A long-time favorite around my house because the ingredients are always handy and it tastes wonderful.

1 lb. red potatoes, sliced
1 T. olive oil
1/2 t. salt

1/8 t. pepper
2 T. grated Parmesan cheese

Toss potatoes with oil and place in an ungreased 13"x9" baking dish. Sprinkle with salt, pepper and cheese. Cover tightly with aluminum foil. Bake at 350 degrees for 45 minutes or until tender. Makes 4 to 6 servings.

Rice Casserole

Jennifer Harter
Fort Worth, TX

This is so yummy served with chicken or turkey.

1 c. green pepper, diced
1 c. onion, diced
2 T. butter
3 c. white rice, uncooked
10-oz. pkg. frozen, chopped
    broccoli

4-oz. can mushroom pieces,
    drained
16-oz. jar pasteurized process
    cheese sauce
2 10-3/4 oz. cans cream of
    mushroom soup

In a medium skillet, sauté pepper and onion with butter. Combine remaining ingredients and onion mixture in a greased 13"x9" baking dish. Bake, covered, at 350 degrees for 30 minutes; uncover, and bake an additional 30 minutes. Makes 10 servings.

Smoky Green Beans

Denise Hazen
Cincinnati, OH

The hickory gives this dish such a hearty flavor.

4 slices hickory-smoked bacon,
   diced
1 sweet onion, diced

24-oz. can green beans,
   undrained
8-oz. can tomato sauce

In a large skillet, brown bacon and onion together for 15 minutes, stirring often. Add beans; stir in tomato sauce. Cover and simmer for one hour. Makes 4 servings.

Decorate an old chair for the garden! Simply wrap grapevine around the chair, tack a birdhouse to the back and place a pretty potted plant on the seat...a delightful garden accent.

Roasted Asparagus

Karen Jones
Manchester, NJ

It's best to use fresh asparagus for this recipe because frozen or canned won't roast well.

1 lb. asparagus
1/2 c. onion, minced
1/2 c. red pepper, sliced
1 T. olive oil

1/8 t. garlic powder
1/2 t. dried rosemary
1/2 T. balsamic vinegar

In a heavy roasting pan, place asparagus, onion and red pepper. Toss with olive oil, garlic and rosemary. Roast, uncovered, at 500 degrees for 10 minutes; drizzle with balsamic vinegar before serving. Makes 4 servings.

Corn syrup is a great way to remove grass stains from clothes. Use it as a prewash stain remover. If the stain doesn't come out the first time, repeat.

Pumpkin Farmer's Casserole

Susan Young
Madison, AL

Easy to prepare for a traditional Thanksgiving flavor, anytime.

15-oz. can pumpkin
12-oz. can evaporated milk
1/4 c. butter, melted
1/2 c. sugar

4 eggs
2 t. cinnamon
1/4 t. nutmeg
1/4 t. ground cloves

Mix all ingredients together in a large mixing bowl. Pour into a lightly greased 2-quart baking dish. Bake, uncovered, at 325 degrees for 45 minutes or until set. Makes 8 servings.

Curried Rice

Dorothy Jackson
Weddington, NC

For a tasty variation, use chicken or shrimp instead of the ground beef.

1 lb. ground beef
1 c. white rice, uncooked
1 T. Worcestershire sauce

2 10-1/2 oz. cans beef broth
2 t. curry powder
1 onion, chopped

In a large skillet, brown ground beef; drain. In a 13"x9" baking dish, combine all ingredients. Cover with aluminum foil and bake at 350 degrees for one hour. Makes 4 to 6 servings.

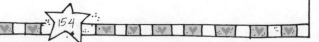

Corn Casserole

Marilyn Just
De Soto, KS

A must-have at any autumn celebration.

1 stick margarine
15-1/4 oz. can corn, drained
14-3/4 oz. can cream-style corn
7-oz. pkg. corn muffin mix
2 eggs, beaten
8 oz. sour cream

Melt margarine in a 13"x9" baking dish in a 350 degree oven. In a large mixing bowl, combine remaining ingredients. When margarine is melted, remove baking dish from oven. Pour corn mixture directly into baking dish with the margarine; combine thoroughly. Bake, uncovered, at 350 degrees for 45 minutes. Makes 8 servings.

Plant a seed of friendship; reap a bouquet of happiness.

-Lois L. Kaufman

Maple Sweet Potatoes

Wendy Paffenroth
Pine Island, NY

Sweet and yummy!

1 t. vanilla extract
1 c. maple syrup
3 T. butter

4 to 5 red apples, sliced
4 to 5 sweet potatoes, boiled
   and sliced

Simmer vanilla and maple syrup in a large saucepan for 5 to
10 minutes; add butter and apples. Cook until the apples are fork
tender; remove from sauce with a slotted spoon. In a greased 2-quart
baking dish, layer apples and potatoes; pour sauce mixture over all.
Bake, covered, at 325 degrees for 20 minutes. Makes 6 servings.

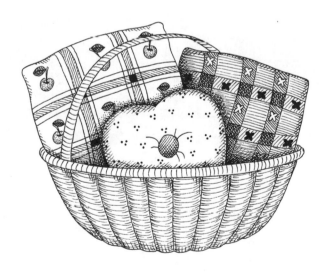

Never store food in a cast iron pot. It could turn the food
black and give it a metallic taste.

Speedy Sides

Cheesy Ranch Potatoes

Dayna Hansen
Junction City, OR

Yummy potatoes with a cheesy twist!

4-oz. pkg. dry buttermilk ranch
  salad dressing mix
1 c. buttermilk
1 c. sour cream

6 to 8 potatoes, boiled and
  chopped
3 c. shredded Cheddar cheese,
  divided

In a small mixing bowl, combine dressing mix with buttermilk and
sour cream. In a large mixing bowl, combine potatoes, 2 cups of
cheese and dressing mixture. Pour mixture into an ungreased
13"x9" baking dish. Top with remaining cheese. Bake, uncovered,
at 350 degrees for 25 to 30 minutes. Makes 8 to 10 servings.

Zucchini Fritters

Melissa Hart
Middleville, MI

Good as a light lunch or a side dish with supper.

2 zucchini, grated
1 egg
2/3 c. shredded Cheddar cheese

2/3 c. round, buttery crackers,
  crumbled
seasoned salt to taste
2 T. oil

Combine zucchini, egg, cheese, crackers and salt in a large mixing
bowl. If mixture seems wet, add extra crackers; shape mixture into
patties. Heat oil in a skillet; fry patties until golden brown, about
3 minutes per side. Makes 4 to 6 servings.

*If your favorite casserole drips in the oven, place a sheet of
foil under the pan to catch drippings...clean up's a snap!*

Family-Favorite Mac & Cheese ▶

Julie Remer
Gahanna, OH

This is a revised version of the macaroni & cheese my mom made for us when we were growing up. She learned how to make it in her high school Home Ec class...now I make it for my kids!

16-oz. pkg. elbow macaroni,
   uncooked
1 egg
1/2 c. butter, divided
1/4 c. all-purpose flour
2-1/2 c. skim milk
2 t. dry mustard

16-oz. pkg. shredded Cheddar
   cheese, divided
1/2 t. seasoned salt
1/2 t. salt
1/2 t. pepper
1-1/2 c. soft bread crumbs,
   divided

Cook macaroni according to package directions; drain and set aside. Meanwhile, beat egg in a medium bowl and set aside. In a large saucepan, melt 1/4 cup butter over medium-low heat. Add flour and cook, whisking constantly, for 5 minutes. Add milk and mustard; whisk until smooth. Continue to cook and whisk until sauce is very thick, 5 to 8 minutes. Reduce heat to low. Remove 1/4 cup of hot milk mixture and slowly add it to the egg, whisking until combined. Pour this mixture back into the saucepan and stir. Set aside 1/2 cup cheese for topping. Add remaining cheese to mixture in saucepan; stir until completely melted. Stir in seasonings and macaroni. Melt remaining butter; toss with bread crumbs. Sprinkle half of crumb mixture into a greased 3-quart casserole dish; spoon in macaroni mixture. Top with remaining crumb mixture and cheese. Cover and bake at 350 degrees for 20 to 25 minutes, until bubbly and golden. Serves 8.

Dorm rooms can be cozy, so a small basket filled with travel-size bath bars, bath oil, beads and herbal shampoo is not only thoughtful, but just the right size to give a student going away to college.

Speedy Sides

Easy Carrot Casserole

Wendy Bush
Morrill, NE

Use fresh carrots for the best flavor!

4 to 5 carrots, chopped
1 c. pasteurized process cheese
   spread, cubed

1/4 c. butter
1/2 onion, finely chopped
3/4 c. potato chips, crushed

In a medium saucepan, cook carrots in salted water about 12 minutes; drain. Stir in cheese, butter and onion. Place mixture into a 2-quart baking dish coated with non-stick vegetable spray; top with potato chips. Bake, uncovered, at 350 degrees for 30 minutes. Makes 6 to 8 servings.

Spinach Casserole

Carrie McNamer
Boston, MA

I like to serve this dish for Sunday dinner...it's always a hit!

2 10-oz. pkgs. frozen, chopped
   spinach, cooked
1-oz. pkg. dry onion soup mix

2 c. sour cream
1/2 c. shredded Colby Jack
   cheese

In a medium mixing bowl, combine spinach, soup mix and sour cream. Spoon into a greased 2-quart casserole dish; top with cheese. Bake, uncovered, at 350 degrees for 25 minutes or until heated through. Makes 8 to 10 servings.

*The kitchen is the heart of the home, and the
mother is queen of the kitchen.*

-Owen Meredith

Baked California Mix

Nancy Geurtz
Kaukauna, WI

To avoid a trip to the store, use whatever vegetables you have in your pantry or freezer.

6-oz. pkg. stuffing mix, cooked
16-oz. pkg. frozen
   California-blend vegetables

10-3/4 oz. can cream of chicken
   soup
8 oz. sour cream

Place stuffing in an ungreased 8"x8" baking dish. Heat vegetables in a microwave-safe dish on high for 4 to 5 minutes or until heated through; layer over stuffing. In a medium mixing bowl, combine soup and sour cream; pour over vegetables. Bake, covered, at 350 degrees for 25 to 35 minutes; uncover and bake an additional 10 minutes. Makes 10 to 12 servings.

Microwaves are great time-savers. Start baked potatoes in the microwave, then finish baking in the oven for a great texture.

Speedy Sides

Twice-Baked Potato Casserole

Emily Hutchins Ellis
Powell, OH

My mom Vickie and I make this casserole for special family occasions. It's easy and the dish always comes home empty!

6 lg. potatoes
1-1/4 t. salt
1/4 t. pepper
1/4 c. butter
1 c. Cheddar cheese, shredded
1 c. hot milk

3 green onions, finely chopped
1/2 c. sour cream
Garnish: Cheddar cheese,
    shredded and green onions,
    chopped

Scrub potatoes. Pierce skins and bake at 425 degrees for 60 minutes. Cut potatoes and scoop out pulp; mash. Add salt, pepper, butter and cheese; beat well. Add hot milk and beat until fluffy and cheese is melted. Stir in green onions and sour cream; blend. Reduce oven temperature to 375 degrees. Spoon potatoes into an 11"x7" baking dish. Sprinkle with cheese and green onions; bake 15 minutes. Makes 6 servings.

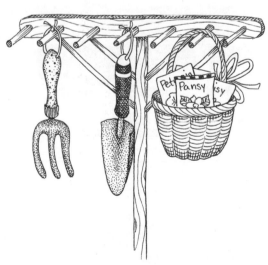

Make store-bought coleslaw your own by adding shredded Cheddar cheese, apple, bell pepper or raisins.

Sweet Brown Rice

Natalie Holdren
Overland Park, KS

*Add dried apricots, dates, figs or prune pieces
for something a little different.*

14-oz. pkg. instant brown rice,
   uncooked
1/2 c. dried cranberries
1/2 c. sunflower seeds

2 T. orange marmalade
1 T. spicy mustard
1-1/2 t. prepared horseradish
1 T. honey

Prepare rice according to package directions; as it simmers add cranberries and sunflower seeds. In a microwave-safe dish, heat marmalade in the microwave for 10 seconds. In a medium mixing bowl, combine marmalade, mustard, horseradish and honey; toss over rice. Makes 9 servings.

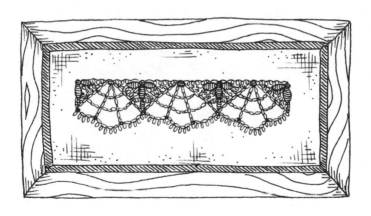

*Frame a piece of old-fashioned lace and some vintage buttons
from your grandmother's sewing box.
What a sweet remembrance!*

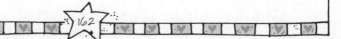

Squash Pie

Charlotte Miles
Statesville, NC

A different way to use your fall squash.

1-1/2 c. sugar
3 eggs, beaten
1/2 stick margarine, melted
1 c. yellow squash, cooked and
   chopped

1 T. self-rising flour
2 t. lemon flavoring
1-1/2 t. coconut flavoring
9-inch pie crust, unbaked

In a large mixing bowl, mix first 7 ingredients together; pour into pie crust. Bake at 350 degrees for 35 to 40 minutes. Makes 8 servings.

Sugared Sweet Potatoes

Patricia Rozzelle
Mineral Bluff, GA

A yummy and easy way to serve sweet potatoes.

1-1/2 c. brown sugar, packed
1/4 c. margarine
3/4 t. salt
1 t. vanilla extract

1 c. cola-flavored carbonated
   drink
9 sweet potatoes, boiled and
   sliced

In a medium saucepan, heat brown sugar, margarine, salt, vanilla and cola; bring to a boil for 5 minutes. Arrange potatoes in an ungreased 13"x9" baking dish. Pour brown sugar mixture over potatoes. Bake, uncovered, at 350 degrees for 25 to 30 minutes or until edges are crisp. Makes 10 to 12 servings.

Mushrooms & Peas Rice

Vickie

My husband and I really enjoy this dish!

8-oz. pkg. sliced mushrooms
1 T. butter
10-3/4 oz. can cream of
   mushroom soup
1 soup can milk

1-3/4 c. instant white rice,
   uncooked
1-1/2 c. frozen peas, thawed
salt and pepper to taste

In a large skillet, sauté mushrooms in butter; set aside. In a large saucepan, heat soup and milk; bring to a boil. Add rice to soup mixture and cover. Let cook for at least 5 minutes. When the rice is tender, stir in mushrooms and peas; salt and pepper. Makes 4 to 6 servings.

Making your own "smoothies" is easy and quick. Fill your blender or food processor with your favorite fresh or frozen fruit. Add juice to taste, or try milk, yogurt or even ice cream. Garnish with a sprig of mint or a slice of lemon.

Speedy Sides

Microwave Applesauce

Tami Bowman
Marysville, OH

There's nothing more special than homemade applesauce.

6 apples, chopped
1/4 c. water
1/3 c. sugar

1/2 t. cinnamon
1/4 t. nutmeg

In a 2-quart microwave-safe dish, combine all ingredients. Microwave on high for 6 to 8 minutes; transfer to a food processor and process until smooth. Makes 6 to 8 servings.

The secret of getting ahead is getting started.

–Mark Twain

Garlic Green Beans

Geneva Rogers
Gillette, WY

My sister shared this recipe with me...it's the only way I can get my kids to eat their green beans.

2 T. butter
3 T. olive oil
1 bulb garlic, chopped

2 14-1/2 oz. cans green beans,
   drained
salt and pepper to taste
1/2 c. grated Parmesan cheese

Melt butter in a large skillet, stir in olive oil and garlic. Sauté over low to medium heat until garlic is slightly browned. Stir in green beans, salt and pepper; cook until beans are heated through. Remove from heat and sprinkle with Parmesan cheese. Makes 4 to 6 servings.

Freeze lemonade in ice cube tray...a clever and refreshing way to chill iced tea!

Speedy Sides

Creamy Cucumbers

Megan Brooks
Antioch, TN

A terrific way to use those extra cucumbers from your garden.

2 T. butter
1/2 c. onion, chopped
1 lb. cucumbers, chopped

1/8 t. pepper
1/2 c. sour cream
1/8 t. dried dill weed

Melt butter in a medium skillet. When butter is melted, add onion and cook over medium heat for 5 minutes. Stir in cucumbers and cook an additional 5 minutes; sprinkle with pepper. Reduce heat to low and stir in sour cream and dill weed. Serve warm. Makes 4 servings.

Easy Steamed Veggies

Linda Berge
Orange, CA

So easy, and clean-up's a breeze.

4 potatoes, sliced
2 zucchini, sliced
2 carrots, sliced
8 to 10 mushrooms, sliced

1 head broccoli, chopped
salt and pepper
6 T. butter

Place even amounts of vegetables into 6 sheets of aluminum foil; salt and pepper to taste. Place one tablespoon butter on top of each vegetable mixture; fold aluminum foil around vegetables. Place packets on baking sheet. Bake at 375 degrees for 40 minutes. Makes 6 servings.

Broccoli with Lemon Sauce

Robin Hill
Rochester, NY

Everyone begs me to bring this dish to family gatherings.

1 bunch broccoli, chopped   1 T. lemon-lime soda
1 T. lemon juice

In a large saucepan, cover broccoli with water; simmer for 12 minutes and drain. Mix together lemon juice and lemon-lime soda; spoon over broccoli. Keep warm until ready to serve. Makes 4 servings.

Add a splash of lemon juice to frozen orange juice...tastes like the orange juice is fresh-squeezed.

Creamed Corn

Sherri Smith
Ravenna, OH

If you have a little extra time, use fresh corn on the cob. Just use the liquid from the corn instead of the milk called for in the recipe.

1 c. canned corn
1/2 t. milk
2 T. sugar
2 slices bacon, crisply cooked, crumbled and drippings reserved

3 T. all-purpose flour
1/2 c. water
salt and pepper to taste

In a medium mixing bowl, combine corn and milk; add sugar. Place corn mixture and bacon drippings in a large skillet. In a measuring cup, mix flour and water together; blend until smooth. Add enough additional water to the measuring cup to equal one cup. Add flour mixture to corn and stir over medium heat until mixture is thick; salt and pepper to taste. Cook for 10 to 15 minutes. Makes 4 to 6 servings.

Friendship is like money: easier made than kept.

–Samuel Butler

Roasted Vegetable Pot

Melody Taynor
Everett, WA

Potatoes, carrots and onions...yummy!

3 c. potatoes, sliced
3 c. carrots, sliced

1/2 c. onion, chopped
15-oz. can beef broth

In a 6-quart slow cooker, combine potatoes, carrots and onion. Pour broth evenly over all. Cover and cook on high for 4 to 6 hours; mix well before serving. Makes 6 to 8 servings.

Super Cranberry Sauce

Karen Uyeda
San Jose, CA

Cranberries are not just for the holiday season...this is tasty all year 'round!

1 c. orange juice
2 c. sugar

3 c. cranberries

In a large saucepan, combine all ingredients. Cook over medium heat, stirring constantly until berries burst. Makes 4 servings.

You see much more of your children once they leave home.

-Lucille Ball

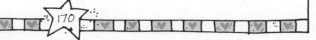

Favorite Baked Beans

Lisa Watkins
Circleville, OH

Just place everything in the slow cooker in the morning, go to work, come home and it's all done.

16-oz. pkg. pinto beans, rinsed
   and drained
3-1/2 c. water
1/2 c. honey
1/4 c. brown sugar, packed

1 onion, chopped
1/4 lb. salt pork, cubed
1 T. mustard
1/2 t. salt

Combine all ingredients in a 6-quart slow cooker. Cover and cook on high for 6 to 7 hours or until beans are tender. Makes 6 servings.

Save the water that the potatoes boiled in...add to soups and sauces to add thickness, nutrition and flavor.

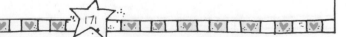

Caramelized Tomatoes

Karen Stoner
Delaware, OH

A good recipe to use up all those abundant garden tomatoes.

6 tomatoes, cored
1/2 t. salt
1/8 t. pepper

2 T. brown sugar, packed
2 T. butter

Arrange tomatoes in an ungreased 13"x9" baking dish; sprinkle with salt, pepper and brown sugar. Dot tops with butter. Bake, uncovered, at 375 degrees for 20 minutes. Makes 6 servings.

Fill an empty spice bottle with toothpicks...then just shake out when needed.

NOTHING TO·IT Desserts

- ☐ Develop film
- ☐ PTA Meeting
- ☐ Buy fresh flowers
- ☐ Get oil changed
- ☐ Sort magazines
- ☐ Order checks
- ☐ Register for computer class
- ☐ Dinner!

"In each day is time for a smile." –Unknown

Buckeye Brownies

Heather Prentice
Mars, PA

Chocolate and peanut butter combined...just like buckeye candies.

19-1/2 oz. pkg. brownie mix
2 c. powdered sugar
1/2 c. plus 6 T. butter, softened
   and divided

8-oz. jar creamy peanut butter
6-oz. pkg. semi-sweet
   chocolate chips

Prepare and bake brownie mix in a greased 13"x9" baking pan according to package directions. Let cool. Mix powdered sugar, 1/2 cup butter and peanut butter. Mix well and spread over cooled brownies. Chill for one hour. Melt together chocolate chips and remaining butter in a saucepan over low heat, stirring occasionally. Spread over brownies. Let cool; cut into squares. Makes 2 to 3 dozen.

Line your brownie dish with aluminum foil...be sure to grease.
After brownies are baked and cooled, they lift right out.
And best of all, clean-up is a breeze!

Creamy No-Bake Pumpkin Pie

DeNeane Deskins
Marengo, OH

Mix, pour and chill...how much easier could it be?

1-1/2 c. milk
6-oz. pkg. instant vanilla
    pudding mix
1 c. canned pumpkin

1 t. pumpkin pie spice
2-1/2 c. whipped topping,
    divided
9-inch pie crust, baked

Combine milk, pudding mix, pumpkin, spice and one cup whipped topping in a large mixing bowl. Beat at low speed for one minute; pour into pie crust. Chill at least 3 hours. Top with remaining whipped topping. Makes 8 servings.

Chocolate Chip-Pudding Cake

Beth Barchesky
Latrobe, PA

My husband likes whipped topping on this cake.

3-1/2 oz. pkg. non-instant
    chocolate pudding mix

18-1/4 oz. pkg. chocolate cake
    mix
12-oz. pkg. chocolate chips

Prepare pudding mix according to package directions. When done, remove from stove top and stir in dry cake mix until just blended. Spread mixture into a greased and floured 13"x9" baking dish. Sprinkle chocolate chips over all. Bake, uncovered, at 325 degrees for 30 to 35 minutes. Makes 14 to 16 servings.

Butter Pecan-Peach Cake

Carole Akers
Bellevue, OH

*So refreshing in the summer, or serve warm on chilly days...
yummy!*

29-oz. can sliced peaches,
   undrained
18-1/4 oz. pkg. butter pecan or
   yellow cake mix

1/2 c. butter, melted
1 c. chopped pecans
1 c. flaked coconut

In the bottom of an ungreased 13"x9" baking pan, pour in peaches and syrup. Cover with dry cake mix; drizzle butter over the top. Sprinkle with pecans and coconut. Bake, uncovered, at 350 degrees for 30 to 35 minutes. Makes 18 to 24 servings.

An easy way to core apples and peaches...slice fruit in half and then use a melon baller to scoop out the core.

Custard Pie

Nina Wallace
Hopkinsville, KY

For a different flavor, add flaked coconut.

4 eggs, divided
1/2 c. sugar
1/4 t. salt
1 t. vanilla extract

2-1/2 c. milk
9-inch pie crust, unbaked
1/4 t. nutmeg

Separate one egg; set egg white aside. In a medium mixing bowl, beat the yolk and remaining eggs until combined; blend in sugar, salt and vanilla. Stir in milk. Beat reserved egg white until soft peaks form; fold into custard mixture. Pour into pie crust. Bake at 350 degrees for 35 to 45 minutes. Cool and sprinkle with nutmeg. Keep refrigerated until ready to serve. Makes 8 servings.

Pumpkin Cake

Tina Knotts
Cable, OH

Sprinkle your serving plate with nutmeg for an added touch of spice.

18-1/4 oz. pkg. spice cake mix
3-1/2 oz. pkg. instant
   butterscotch pudding mix
4 eggs
1/4 c. water

1/4 c. oil
1-1/2 c. canned pumpkin
2 t. pumpkin pie spice
Garnish: powdered sugar

In a large mixing bowl, blend all ingredients together. Beat at low speed for 30 seconds then 4 minutes on medium speed. Pour into a greased and floured Bundt® pan. Bake at 350 degrees for 45 to 55 minutes or until tested done. Let cool for 30 minutes, then turn out onto a serving plate. When cool, sprinkle with powdered sugar. Makes 8 to 10 servings.

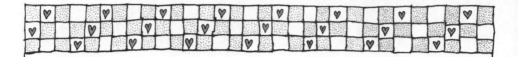

Sweet Coconut Cookies

Deanna Mann
Mesa, AZ

The maple in these cookies reminds me of fall in New England.

1 c. brown sugar, packed
1 c. shortening
1 egg
1 t. maple flavoring
2-1/4 c. all-purpose flour

1/2 t. baking powder
1/2 t. salt
4-oz. can flaked coconut
2 c. sugar

In a large mixing bowl, beat brown sugar, shortening, egg and maple flavoring until fluffy. Add flour, baking powder and salt; mix well. Stir in coconut. Drop by tablespoonfuls 2 inches apart on a greased baking sheet. Dip the bottom of a greased glass into sugar and press cookies flat. Bake at 350 degrees for 10 to 12 minutes. Makes 5 to 6 dozen cookies.

Life is unsure...eat dessert first!

-Anonymous

3-2-1 Lemon Cookies

Sharon Hill
Roanoke, IL

When I first saw this recipe, I thought that it was a joke...it sounded so odd. Give 'em a try, they're delicious!

3 eggs	8 oz. whipped topping
2 18-1/4 oz. pkgs. lemon cake mix	1 c. powdered sugar

In a large mixing bowl, combine eggs, cake mixes and whipped topping; mix well. Chill dough for at least one hour. Drop by tablespoonfuls into powdered sugar; coat thoroughly and roll into balls. Place balls on a greased baking sheet. Bake at 375 degrees for 10 minutes. Makes 8 dozen cookies.

Keep your cookies moist! Place one slice of bread into a cookie jar or the storage bag and your treats will stay soft.

Root Beer Float Cake

Mary Patenaude
Norwich, CT

Easy to make and it tastes just like a cool root beer float.

18-1/4 oz. pkg. white cake mix
2-1/4 c. chilled root beer,
   divided

1/4 c. oil
2 eggs
1 envelope whipped topping mix

In a large mixing bowl, combine cake mix, 1-1/4 cup root beer, oil and eggs together; beat until well blended. Pour into a greased 13"x9" baking pan. Bake, uncovered, at 350 degrees for 30 to 35 minutes; cool completely. In a medium mixing bowl, combine whipped topping mix and remaining root beer; beat until soft peaks form. Frost cake. Makes 24 servings.

If you're trying to invert a cake and it just won't come out of the baking dish, place a warm, damp towel over the bottom of the inverted pan until the cake loosens.

Raspberry Cream Pie

Jennifer Barga
Dublin, OH

Use blackberries instead of raspberries for a sweet change.

14-oz. can sweetened condensed
  milk
2/3 c. frozen raspberry-
  lemonade concentrate,
  thawed

8 oz. whipped topping
1 c. frozen raspberries, divided
9-inch graham cracker pie crust

In a large mixing bowl, combine milk and concentrate; mix well.
Fold in whipped topping. Spoon 1/2 cup raspberries into the bottom
of crust; top with filling and chill for 6 hours. Top with remaining
raspberries before serving. Makes 8 servings.

Busy Day Lemon Cheesecake

Brenda Erwin
Hurricane, WV

Tart, sweet...a special treat!

8-oz. pkg. cream cheese
2 c. milk, divided

3-1/2 oz. pkg. instant lemon
  pudding mix
9-inch graham cracker pie crust

In a large mixing bowl, stir cream cheese with a fork until creamy.
Add 1/2 cup milk, a small amount at a time, blending until mixture is
very smooth. Add remaining milk and pudding mix. Beat with whisk
for about one minute or until well mixed; pour into crust. Chill for one
hour. Makes 8 servings.

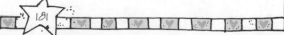

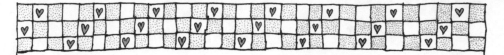

Mile-High Coconut Cream Pie

Amy Butcher
Columbus, GA

Just like Grandmother used to make!

1 c. sweetened flaked coconut
9-inch pie crust, baked and
   cooled
1 c. sugar

1/4 c. cornstarch
3 egg yolks, beaten
2-1/4 c. whole milk
1 t. vanilla extract

Sprinkle coconut in crust; set aside. Stir together sugar and cornstarch. Place egg yolks in a medium heavy saucepan; whisk in sugar mixture and milk alternately until smooth. Cook and stir over medium-high heat until boiling and thickened, about 10 to 15 minutes. Remove from heat and stir in vanilla; pour over coconut in crust. Spoon meringue over hot filling, sealing carefully to edge of crust. Bake at 325 degrees until meringue is lightly golden, 15 to 20 minutes. Serves 8.

Meringue:

5 to 6 egg whites
1/4 t. cream of tartar

6 T. sugar
1/2 t. vanilla extract

In a deep bowl, beat egg whites with an electric mixer on high speed until soft peaks form. Reduce mixer to low speed; add cream of tartar. Gradually beat in sugar, one tablespoon at a time; beat until stiff, glossy peaks form. Beat in vanilla.

Make your cookies all the same size! Use a mini ice cream scoop to drop dough onto baking sheets, or roll dough into a log, chill and slice.

Country Harvest Pie

Janis Parr
Ontario, Canada

This pie looks and tastes amazing. The cranberries give it color and complement the sweet mellowness of the apples and pears. Everyone loves it!

2 9-inch pie crusts
3 McIntosh apples, peeled, cored
   and thickly sliced
3 Bartlett pears, peeled, cored
   and sliced
3/4 c. fresh cranberries
3/4 c. sugar

3 T. all-purpose flour
1/4 t. cinnamon
1 T. milk
2 t. butter, sliced
Optional: whipped cream or
   vanilla ice cream

Place one pie crust in a 9" pie plate; set aside. In a large bowl, combine apples, pears, cranberries and sugar; set aside. In a small bowl, mix together flour and cinnamon; combine with fruit mixture. Sprinkle milk over fruit mixture; stir well. Spoon into pie crust; dot with butter. Add top crust; crimp edges and cut several vents. Bake at 425 degrees for 15 minutes. Reduce oven to 350 degrees and continue baking for 35 to 45 minutes, until apples are tender. Garnish with whipped cream or ice cream, if desired. Serves 6 to 8.

Mini tarts are just right after a hearty dinner. With a 4-inch biscuit cutter, cut 6 circles from a pie crust. Press gently into ungreased muffin cups. Spoon 2 tablespoons apple or cherry pie filling into each cup. Bake at 425 degrees for 14 to 18 minutes, until bubbly and golden. So sweet!

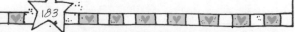

Pecan Pie Bars

Phyllis Drew
Madison, SD

Delectable...and it's my little secret how easy they are to make!

18-1/2 oz. pkg. yellow cake mix, divided
1/2 c. butter, melted
1 egg, beaten
1/2 c. brown sugar, packed

1-1/2 c. light corn syrup
3 eggs, beaten
1 t. vanilla extract
1 c. chopped pecans

Set aside 2/3 cup dry cake mix for filling. In a large bowl, combine remaining cake mix, butter and egg; mix well. Press into a greased 13"x9" baking pan. Bake at 350 degrees for 15 to 20 minutes, until lightly golden; remove and set aside. In a large bowl, combine reserved cake mix, brown sugar, corn syrup, eggs and vanilla. Beat for 2 minutes with an electric mixer on medium speed. Stir in pecans and pour over baked crust. Bake for 30 to 35 minutes at 350 degrees, until almost set. Cool; slice into bars. Makes about 2 dozen.

Plump up and add flavor to raisins. Place raisins in a saucepan and cover with cold water. Bring to a boil, then remove from heat and let sit for 5 minutes. Drain and pat dry.

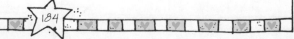

Taffy Apple Cupcakes

Angie Biggins
Lyons, IL

What fun...a gooey caramel-topped cupcake on a stick!

18-1/4 oz. pkg. carrot cake mix
1 c. Granny Smith apples, cored, peeled and finely chopped
1/2 t. cinnamon
20 caramels, unwrapped

1/4 c. milk
1 c. pecans or walnuts, finely chopped
12 wooden craft sticks

Prepare cake mix according to package instructions; stir in apples and cinnamon. Fill paper-lined jumbo muffin cups 2/3 full. Bake at 350 degrees for 20 to 25 minutes, until a toothpick inserted near center tests clean. Combine caramels and milk in a small saucepan over low heat; stir until melted and smooth. Drizzle caramel over cooled cupcakes; sprinkle nuts over top. Insert a craft stick into center of each cupcake. Makes one dozen.

A quick and soothing way to calm an upset stomach...place 1/2 to 3/4 of a teaspoon of cinnamon into a mugful of boiling water and stir. Yum!

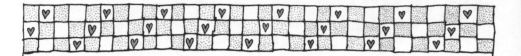

Quick Blueberry Crisp

Flo Burtnett
Gage, OK

Try with cherry pie filling, too.

21-oz. can blueberry pie filling
1/2 c. rolled oats, uncooked
1/2 c. all-purpose flour

1/4 c. brown sugar, packed
2 T. chopped walnuts
6 T. margarine

Spoon blueberry pie filling into a one-quart baking dish coated with non-stick vegetable spray. In a medium mixing bowl, combine oats, flour, brown sugar and walnuts. With a pastry blender or 2 knives, cut in margarine until mixture resembles coarse crumbs. Sprinkle over pie filling. Bake, uncovered, at 375 degrees for 45 minutes or until lightly browned and bubbly. Makes 4 to 6 servings.

If a blueberry recipe calls for buttermilk, substitute regular milk...if it calls for baking soda, use baking powder. This will keep the blueberries from discoloring muffins, breads or desserts.

Microwave Peanut Brittle

Susie Montag
Richlands, NC

A microwave dessert...homemade in minutes. How easy!

1-1/2 c. roasted peanuts
1 c. sugar
1/2 c. corn syrup
1/2 t. salt

1 T. butter
1 t. vanilla extract
1 t. baking soda

In a large microwave-safe bowl, mix peanuts, sugar, corn syrup and salt. Cook on high for 6 to 7 minutes; mixture should be bubbly and peanuts lightly browned. Quickly stir in butter and vanilla; cook 2 to 3 additional minutes. Add baking soda and stir quickly until mixture is foamy. Pour immediately onto a greased baking sheet. Let cool for 15 minutes or longer. Break into pieces and store in an airtight container. Makes 14 to 16 servings.

When shipping cookies, place pieces of wax paper between cookie layers and add mini marshmallows to make sure cookies don't move around. Tuck in a couple packages of cocoa for a great gift.

Shortbread Cookies

Cathy Unrein
Windsor, CO

A melt-in-your-mouth treat!

1 c. sugar
1 c. shortening
3 eggs
2 t. cream of tartar

2 t. baking soda
3 c. all-purpose flour
1 t. vanilla extract

Beat sugar and shortening together in a large mixing bowl; add eggs and beat well. Add remaining ingredients and combine. Knead dough into a ball, roll out to 1/4-inch thickness and cut out with your favorite cookie cutter. Place on an ungreased baking sheet. Bake at 350 degrees for 10 to 12 minutes. Makes 3 dozen cookies.

Graham Cracker Cookies

Gayle Wagner
Island Lake, IL

Let the kids pick their favorite toppings...cookie crumbles, candy bars or peanut butter chips to add to this yummy recipe.

20 to 25 graham crackers
1/2 c. sugar
1/2 c. butter
1/2 c. margarine

3/4 c. chopped nuts
3/4 c. chocolate chips
3/4 c. chocolate candy-covered
    pieces

Place graham crackers in a single layer on a baking sheet coated with non-stick vegetable spray. In a medium saucepan, melt sugar, butter and margarine; boil for about 4 minutes. Pour mixture over graham crackers; sprinkle with remaining toppings. Bake at 350 degrees for 10 minutes. Remove and cool on wax paper. Makes 2 dozen cookies.

Mexican Wedding Cookies

Jackie-Jo Cunningham
Glen Rose, TX

The American version of this cookie is known as the snowball.

1 c. butter, softened
2 c. all-purpose flour
1 t. vanilla extract

1 c. powdered sugar
1 c. walnuts, finely chopped
Garnish: powdered sugar

In a large mixing bowl, combine all ingredients; roll into 1-1/2 inch balls. Place on an ungreased baking sheet. Bake at 350 degrees for about 10 to 15 minutes. Roll in powdered sugar while warm. Makes about 3-1/2 dozen.

Keep an eye out for unique cookie cutters...tie a nametag on
to use for placecards, to cut tea sandwiches, or
to add whimsy to garlands.

Easiest Chocolate Mousse

Hilary Kanwischer
Loxahatchee, FL

Serve in tall or fluted glasses garnished with a twist of orange peel.

16 oz. whipped topping
3-1/2 oz. pkg. instant chocolate
    pudding mix

1 to 2 T. cold milk

In a large mixing bowl, combine whipped topping and pudding mix together; add milk slowly. Be sure to keep chilled for best results. Makes 10 servings.

Pound Cake S'mores

Cindy Schmitt
Oelwein, IA

This is the easiest and quickest dessert!

1 baked pound cake, sliced
1 to 2 c. mini marshmallows
12-oz. pkg. semi-sweet
    chocolate chips

12-oz. jar caramel ice cream
    topping
1/2 to 1 c. chopped walnuts

Place cake slices on an ungreased baking sheet; sprinkle with marshmallows and chocolate chips. Broil 4 to 6 inches from the heat source for 2 to 3 minutes or until marshmallows are lightly browned. Transfer 2 slices each to 6 to 8 serving plates and drizzle with caramel topping; sprinkle with walnuts. Makes 6 to 8 servings.

Hot Milk Sponge Cake

Angie Kister
Dover, PA

*This recipe was from my husband's great-great grandmother.
Top it with any kind of icing or just eat plain.*

5 eggs
2 c. all-purpose flour
2 c. sugar
2 t. baking powder

1 c. milk
1 T. butter
2 t. vanilla extract

In a medium mixing bowl, beat eggs, flour, sugar, baking powder and salt together. In a medium saucepan, heat milk and butter together; add egg mixture and vanilla. Pour batter into a greased and floured 13"x9" baking dish. Bake at 375 degrees for about 30 to 40 minutes or until tested done. Makes 12 to 14 servings.

Muffins bake more evenly if you fill one muffin tin with water. It also prevents burning and makes it easier to remove the muffins from the pan.

Giant Cream Puffs ▶

Virginia Watson
Scranton, PA

Watch everyone line up for one of the best old-fashioned sweet treats around! Cream puffs can also be filled with any flavor of ice cream, custard or pudding.

1 c. water
1/2 c. butter
1 c. all-purpose flour
1/4 t. salt

3 eggs
Garnish: powdered sugar or
    melted chocolate

Combine water and butter in a large heavy saucepan; bring to a boil. Remove from heat; stir until butter melts. Add flour and salt; mix thoroughly until dough comes away from sides of saucepan. Add eggs one at a time, beating well after each. Place dough in a pastry bag fitted with a large plain tip (or use a large spoon). Form 8 rounds on parchment paper-lined baking sheets; smooth tops with a finger dipped in cold water. Bake at 400 degrees for 30 to 35 minutes, until golden. Let stand for several minutes in oven with oven door open; cool on a wire rack. Slice puffs open; fill with Cream Filling. Garnish as desired with a sprinkle of powdered sugar or a drizzle of melted chocolate. Serve within one hour. Makes 8 puffs.

Cream Filling:

3-1/2 oz. pkg. instant French
    vanilla pudding mix

1 c. milk
1 c. whipping cream

In a medium bowl, beat pudding mix and milk together with an electric mixer on medium-high speed; set aside. In a separate bowl, beat whipping cream until soft peaks form. Gently fold whipped cream into pudding mixture. Chill.

German Chocolate Brownies

Patty Fosnight
Channelview, TX

Serve with ice cream on top.

1 c. sugar
1/2 c. all-purpose flour
3 eggs

1 c. chopped pecans
1 stick butter
2 oz. German chocolate

In a medium mixing bowl, combine sugar, flour, eggs and pecans; set aside. In a small saucepan, melt butter and chocolate, stirring constantly. Pour chocolate mixture into sugar mixture; blend well. Pour into a lightly greased 9-inch pie pan. Bake, uncovered, at 350 degrees for 30 minutes or until tested done. Makes 8 servings.

Add the finishing touches to brownies with a sprinkle of powdered sugar, then top with chocolate curls or colorful, candy-coated chocolate pieces.

Skillet Fruit Cobbler

Michelle Campen
Peoria, IL

Use your favorite fruit in this recipe...whatever you choose, it's delicious!

1 stick margarine
1 c. all-purpose flour
1-1/4 c. sugar
3/4 c. milk
1 qt. canned fruit

Melt margarine in an oven-proof skillet. In a medium mixing bowl, sift together flour and sugar; stir in milk. Pour into skillet over margarine; add fruit. Bake, uncovered, at 325 degrees for 45 minutes or until browned. Makes 6 to 8 servings.

Nutty Buddy Pie

Vickie

A frozen summertime dessert.

8-oz. pkg. cream cheese,
    softened
2 c. powdered sugar
1 c. milk
1 c. crunchy peanut butter
16 oz. whipped topping
3 9-inch chocolate pie crusts
1-1/4 c. chopped peanuts
Garnish: chocolate syrup

In a large mixing bowl, beat together cream cheese, powdered sugar, milk and peanut butter; blend in whipped topping. Divide equally between pie crusts; sprinkle with peanuts. Drizzle chocolate syrup over all. Cover and freeze at least 3 hours or longer. Remove from freezer 15 to 20 minutes before serving. Serves 24 to 28.

Chocolate-Peanut Butter Fudge

Cindy Bartels
Scranton, PA

The peanut butter in this recipe makes it extra special.

4 c. powdered sugar
1/4 t. salt
1/4 c. baking cocoa
1 t. vanilla extract

1-1/4 c. creamy or chunky
   peanut butter
1-1/4 c. butter, melted

In a large mixing bowl, mix together powdered sugar, salt, cocoa and vanilla. Add peanut butter. Pour butter over top; mix well. Line a 13"x9" pan with plastic wrap; press fudge mixture into pan, smooth out top, cut and refrigerate. Makes about 75 fudge pieces.

For a quick summertime treat, combine blueberries and an equal amount of sugar in a saucepan over low heat until thickened. Let cool and pour over softened vanilla ice cream.

Mimi's Sugar Cookies

Valerie Hugus
Circleville, OH

Every time my grandmother, Mimi, would come visit, she always made these cookies for us.

2 c. shortening
2-1/4 c. sugar, divided
2 eggs
4 c. all-purpose flour

1 t. cream of tartar
1 t. baking soda
1/8 t. salt
2 t. vanilla extract

In a large mixing bowl, cream shortening and 2 cups sugar together; add eggs. Mix in flour, cream of tartar, baking soda, salt and vanilla. Roll mixture into balls; coat with remaining sugar. Place on an ungreased baking sheet and flatten with a greased glass dipped in sugar. Bake at 350 degrees for 10 minutes. Makes 2 to 3 dozen.

Getting ready to make sugar cookies? Try rolling out the dough on powdered sugar instead of flour...it adds a sweet, yummy taste.

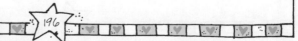

Pound Cake in a Hurry

Beth Purcell
Jacksonville, NC

Serve with fresh strawberries, raspberries or blueberries.

18-1/4 oz. pkg. white cake mix
8 oz. sour cream
3-1/2 oz. pkg. instant vanilla
    pudding mix

4 eggs
1 c. oil

In a large mixing bowl, cream all ingredients together and pour into a greased and floured Bundt® pan. Bake at 350 degrees for 45 to 50 minutes. Makes 10 servings.

Caramel Sauce

Sarina Quaderer
Friendship, WI

Tastes great on pound cake, shortbread and ice cream.

1 c. brown sugar, packed
1/2 c. whipping cream
1/4 c. corn syrup

1 T. butter
2 t. cinnamon

In a large saucepan, heat all ingredients to boiling, stirring constantly. Reduce heat and simmer, uncovered, for about 5 minutes. Makes 1-1/2 cups sauce.

An easy-going husband is the one
indispensable comfort of life.

−Ouida

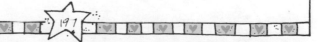

Brown Sugar Pie

Alta Smith
Richmond, VA

There's only one way to describe this pie...mouth-watering!

3 eggs
3 c. brown sugar, packed
3 T. all-purpose flour
1/2 c. butter

1 c. milk
1 t. vanilla extract
2 9-inch pie crusts, unbaked

In a large mixing bowl, combine eggs, brown sugar, flour, butter and milk together; add vanilla. Pour into pie crusts. Bake at 350 degrees for 35 to 45 minutes. Makes 16 servings.

Pineapple Quickie Pie

Michelle Campen
Peoria, IL

A quick and refreshing springtime pie.

20-oz. can crushed pineapple,
   undrained
3-oz. pkg. instant vanilla
   pudding mix

8 oz. whipped topping
9-inch pie crust, baked

Combine pineapple, juice and pudding mix in a medium mixing bowl. Fold in whipped topping. Pour mixture into pie crust; refrigerate for at least 3 hours. Makes 8 servings.

Honeycomb Coffee Cake

Debbie Frye
Hampton Bays, NY

The perfect breakfast or after school treat.

12-oz. tube refrigerated biscuits
1/2 c. graham cracker crumbs
1/2 c. brown sugar, packed

1/4 c. margarine, melted
1 T. lemon juice
1/4 c. honey

Cut biscuits into quarters. Toss in cracker crumbs; place in a 9" pie plate coated with non-stick vegetable spray. Press end of wooden spoon into each piece of biscuit to make a honeycomb effect; sprinkle with brown sugar. In a small mixing bowl, combine margarine and lemon juice; drizzle over biscuits. Bake, uncovered, at 400 degrees for 15 minutes or until lightly browned. Drizzle honey over top of cake while still hot. Makes 8 to 10 servings.

Make chopped walnuts and pecans by placing whole nuts into a plastic zipping bag and pounding with a meat mallet until desired size.

Super Rich Cake

Crystal Cull
Montgomery, IL

We always have this for family birthdays.

18-1/4 oz. pkg. German chocolate cake mix
14-oz. can sweetened condensed milk
17-oz. jar butterscotch-caramel ice cream topping
8 oz. whipped topping
6-oz. bar chocolate covered toffee candy, crushed

Bake cake mix in a greased 13"x9" pan according to package directions. Let cool for 10 minutes, then make holes in cake with wooden spoon handle. Pour milk over top; cover with ice cream topping. When completely cooled, frost with whipped topping and sprinkle with candy bar pieces. Refrigerate until ready to serve. Makes 18 to 24 servings.

When a chocolate cake recipe calls for the pan to be greased and floured, use cocoa instead of flour. The cocoa will keep a white ring from forming around the cake.

Dewberry Cobbler

Gloria Robertson
Midland, TX

If you can't find dewberries, use blackberries instead.

2-1/2 c. dewberries
1 c. sugar
3 T. all-purpose flour
3 T. butter

1/2 t. salt
1/4 t. cinnamon
9-inch pie crust, unbaked and
  torn into strips

In a large mixing bowl, combine dewberries and remaining ingredients, except pie crust, together; pour into a lightly greased 2-quart baking dish. Cover dewberry mixture with pie crust strips. Bake, uncovered, at 425 degrees for 30 minutes or until pie crust is browned. Makes 4 servings.

Popcorn Bars

Jen Sell
Farmington, MN

An easy treat for sleepovers and kids' parties.

1/2 c. margarine
1/2 c. oil
2 10-1/2 oz. pkgs. mini
  marshmallows
2/3 c. popcorn, unpopped

2 c. salted peanuts
12-oz. pkg. colorful,
  candy-coated chocolate
  mini-baking bits

In a large saucepan, melt margarine, oil and marshmallows together over low heat. Pop the popcorn and mix into marshmallow mixture; fold in peanuts and baking bits. Place mixture into 2 greased jelly roll pans. When cool, cut into squares and serve. Makes 18 to 20 servings.

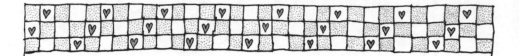

Summer Delight

Terry Zaccuri
Costa Mesa, CA

Very light and delicate.

8-oz. carton strawberry yogurt
1 pt. strawberries, sliced

8 oz. whipped topping
1 baked angel food cake, cubed

In a large serving bowl, mix together yogurt, strawberries and whipped topping. Add angel food cake and stir. Refrigerate for 2 hours. Makes 6 servings.

Banana Bread Trifle

Joanna Gibson
Fort Polk, LA

The taste of Grandma's banana bread in a trifle.

1 loaf banana bread, cubed
5-1/4 oz. pkg. instant vanilla
    pudding mix, prepared
2 to 3 bananas, sliced

12 oz. whipped topping
Garnish: whipped topping and
    chopped nuts

In a trifle bowl, layer half of bread, pudding, bananas and whipped topping; repeat to fill bowl. Top with whipped topping and sprinkle nuts over all; refrigerate until ready to serve. Makes 10 to 12 servings.

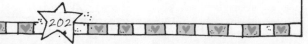

Mallow Cake

MaryAnn Fearby
Medina, NY

Expect the top of this cake to be bubbly and delectably sticky!

4 c. mini marshmallows   21-oz. can cherry pie filling
18-1/4 oz. pkg. yellow cake mix

Layer marshmallows evenly across the bottom of a 13"x9" baking dish coated with non-stick vegetable spray. Prepare cake batter according to package directions and pour over marshmallows. Spoon pie filling over cake batter. Bake, uncovered, at 350 degrees for 45 to 50 minutes. Makes 14 to 16 servings.

Glass or dark baking pans will retain more heat than shiny ones. Be sure to reduce the oven temperature by 25 degrees when using them.

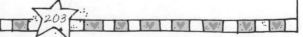

Old-Fashioned Sugar Cream Pie

Donna Zink
Lapeer, MI

Such a simple, but delicious pie.

2-1/4 T. all-purpose flour
1/2 c. sugar
1/2 c. brown sugar, packed

9-inch pie crust, unbaked
1-1/2 c. milk

Stir flour and sugars together in pie crust. Pour milk over all. Bake at 450 degrees for 10 minutes; reduce heat to 350 and bake an additional 35 minutes. Makes 8 servings.

Pumpkin Trifle

Peg Baker
La Rue, OH

I always make this on the first chilly night in autumn.

3 c. baked, unfrosted spice cake,
   crumbled and divided
16-oz. can pumpkin
2-1/2 t. pumpkin pie spice
2-1/2 c. cold milk

4 3-1/2 oz. pkgs. instant
   butterscotch pudding mix
2 c. whipping cream
Garnish: maraschino cherries

Set aside 1/4 cup of the cake crumbs for topping. Divide remaining crumbs into 4 portions; sprinkle one portion of crumbs into the bottom of a trifle bowl. In a large mixing bowl, combine pumpkin, spice, milk and pudding mix; mix until smooth. Spoon half into the trifle bowl. Sprinkle with the second portion of crumbs. Whip cream until stiff; spoon half into the bowl. Sprinkle with the third portion of crumbs and remaining whipped cream. Sprinkle the reserved crumbs around the inside edge of bowl. Top with cherries. Cover and chill for 2 hours. Makes 12 to 15 servings.

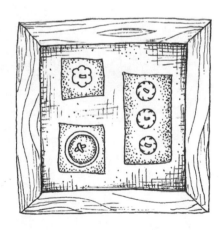

Nothing To It Desserts

Five-Minute Fudge

Jan Prior
Grand Island, NE

This recipe reminds me of my dad...he always made fudge at Christmastime.

2/3 c. evaporated milk
1-2/3 c. sugar
1/2 t. salt
2 c. mini marshmallows

1-1/2 c. chocolate chips
1 t. vanilla extract
1/2 c. chopped walnuts

Mix milk, sugar and salt together in a large saucepan over low heat. Heat to boiling, then cook 5 minutes, stirring constantly. Remove from heat and add marshmallows, chocolate chips, vanilla and walnuts. Stir for one to 2 minutes or until marshmallows melt. Pour into a greased 8"x8" baking pan; chill until firm. Makes 16 servings.

Quick fix! To keep a mixing bowl from sliding around, simply place a damp dishcloth underneath.

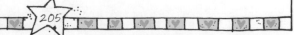

Grasshopper Pie

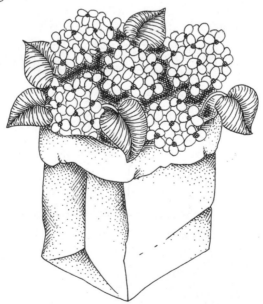

Caryn Dubelko
Dayton, OH

If you don't want to use liqueur, add mint extract and a couple drops of green food coloring.

24 chocolate sandwich cookies, crushed and divided
1/4 c. margarine, melted
1/4 c. creme de menthe liqueur

7-1/2 oz. jar marshmallow creme
2 c. whipping cream, whipped

In a medium mixing bowl, combine 3/4 of cookie crumbs and margarine; press into a greased 9" springform pan. In a medium mixing bowl, gradually add creme de menthe to marshmallow creme, mixing until well blended. Fold in cream; pour into pan. Sprinkle with remaining crumbs and freeze for 2 to 3 hours. Makes 8 servings.

Chill the beaters and mixing bowl to speed up the whipping time for cream.

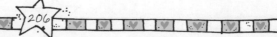

Quick Coffee Cake

Shari Hepner
Lebanon, OH

A family favorite...we make it on special mornings like Christmas.

1 c. oil
2 eggs, beaten
1 t. vanilla extract
1 c. milk
1 c. sugar
3 c. all-purpose flour

3 t. baking powder
1/2 t. salt
1-1/2 c. brown sugar, packed
2 t. cinnamon
1/2 c. chopped walnuts
1 stick margarine, melted

In a large mixing bowl, combine oil, eggs, vanilla and milk together. In a medium mixing bowl, blend together sugar, flour, baking powder and salt; combine with egg mixture. Pour half of batter into a greased 13"x9" baking dish. In a medium mixing bowl, prepare streusel by combining brown sugar, cinnamon and walnuts. Sprinkle half of streusel on top of batter. Top with remaining batter; sprinkle with remaining streusel. Drizzle with margarine. Bake, uncovered, at 350 degrees for 25 to 30 minutes. Makes 18 to 24 servings.

Normal is in the eye
of the beholder.

-Whoopi Goldberg

Cricket Crunchies

Cricket Hansen
West Jordan, UT

My signature treats...I give them to everyone around the holidays.

1 egg white
2 c. chopped pecans

1/4 c. sugar
1 T. cinnamon

In a medium mixing bowl, combine egg white and pecans together until coated and sticky. In a small mixing bowl, combine sugar and cinnamon; sprinkle over pecans, stirring until nuts are evenly coated. Spread pecans on an ungreased baking sheet. Bake at 350 degrees for 30 minutes; remove from oven and cool for 5 minutes. Break apart and store in an air-tight container. Makes 2 cups.

Crispy Treats

Lori Marcar
San Jose, CA

Your kids will love these as an after school snack.

5 c. crispy rice cereal
40 marshmallows

1/2 t. cinnamon
1 c. chopped walnuts

In a large saucepan over low heat, mix all ingredients together. Pour mixture into a greased 13"x9" baking dish. Refrigerate until set; cut into squares. Makes 16 to 18 servings.

Before pressing crispy treats into a baking dish, run fingers under cold water. This will keep the treats from sticking to your hands.

Chocolate-Butterscotch Cookies

Michelle Lamp
Slayton, MN

Whip these up in no time. They're perfect with a chilled glass of milk.

1 c. corn syrup
1 c. sugar
1 c. creamy peanut butter
6 c. crispy rice cereal

6-oz. pkg. semi-sweet chocolate chips
6-oz. pkg. butterscotch chips

In a large saucepan, cook corn syrup and sugar over medium heat, stirring frequently, until mixture comes to a boil; remove from heat. Stir in peanut butter and cereal. Press mixture into a greased 13"x9" baking dish. In a double boiler, melt chocolate and butterscotch chips, stirring constantly, until smooth. Spread mixture over cereal mixture. Refrigerate for 15 minutes. Makes 48 bars.

A quick way to test an egg for freshness...place the egg into a pan of cool, salted water. If the egg sinks, it's fresh; if it rises to the surface, toss it out!

Chocolate-Almond Candy

Melinda Jones
Senath, MO

Candy made in a slow cooker...so easy!

1 T. oil
3 T. unsweetened baking cocoa
24 oz. white almond bark
12-oz. pkg. chocolate chips

16 oz. unsalted, dry roasted
  peanuts
16 oz. salted, dry roasted
  peanuts

Place oil, cocoa, white almond bark and chocolate chips in a 5-quart slow cooker. Cook over high heat until chocolate is melted and smooth; unplug and add peanuts, stir well. Drop by teaspoonfuls onto wax paper; cool. Makes about 8 dozen candies.

To thicken cherry pies, use tapioca instead of cornstarch. High acid fruits can cause cornstarch to fail.

Lemonade Fluff Dessert

Pam Powell
Burlington, IA

This is such a fun dessert to serve on a hot summer day.

70 round, buttery crackers, crushed
1 stick butter, melted
1/4 c. powdered sugar
6-oz. can frozen lemonade, thawed

14-oz. can sweetened condensed milk
16 oz. whipped topping
1-1/2 T. lemon juice

Combine crackers, butter and powdered sugar together; reserve 2/3 cup for topping. Press remaining mixture into an ungreased 13"x9" baking pan. In a separate mixing bowl, combine lemonade, milk, whipped topping and lemon juice; spread over crust. Top with remaining cracker mixture. Refrigerate for 2 to 3 hours. Makes 14 to 16 servings.

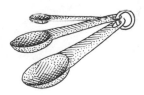

Chocolate Ice Box Pie

Pam Miller
Boise, ID

Decorate with chocolate curls or sprinkles.

4-oz. bar chocolate candy
12 oz. whipped topping

1 chocolate pie crust

In a microwave-safe dish, melt chocolate bar in the microwave. Fold in whipped topping. Place chocolate mixture into pie crust; chill. Makes 6 to 8 servings.

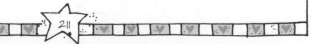

Speedy Little Devils

Cathy Silvast
Greenfield, WI

The kids just love the creamy peanut butter and marshmallow filling.

18-1/4 oz. pkg. devil's food cake mix
1 stick margarine, melted

3/4 c. creamy peanut butter
13-oz. jar marshmallow creme

In a large mixing bowl, thoroughly blend cake mix and margarine. Remove 1/2 cup cake mixture from mixing bowl and set aside for topping. Place remaining mixture in a lightly greased 13"x9" baking dish. Mix peanut butter and marshmallow creme together; spread onto crumb mixture. Sprinkle reserved cake mix over all. Bake at 350 degrees for 20 minutes. Makes 12 to 14 servings.

Non-stick vegetable spray can usually be used instead of shortening to prepare baking sheets and baking dishes.

Yummy Chocolate Crunch

Rebecca Santelli
Mechanicsville, VA

So easy to bring along to parties, or even into work.

1 sleeve saltine crackers	1 c. butter
1 c. sugar	12-oz. pkg. chocolate chips

Place crackers, side by side, in a 13"x9" baking dish lined with aluminum foil, until bottom of dish is covered. In a small saucepan, bring sugar and butter to a boil; stir for 3 minutes while boiling. Pour mixture over the crackers and spread with a spatula until all crackers are covered. Bake at 350 degrees for 10 to 15 minutes or until edges of crackers are golden brown. Immediately remove from oven, spread chocolate chips over all until melted. Freeze for 2 hours. Break into pieces. Makes 12 to 14 servings.

I'm not going to vacuum 'til Sears makes one you can ride on.

-Roseanne Barr

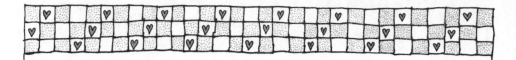

Sundown Cobbler

Holly Young
Concord, NC

What a tempting layered dessert!

1 stick margarine
1 c. self-rising flour
1 c. sugar

1 c. milk
2 to 2-1/2 c. sliced peaches

Melt margarine in a 2-quart baking dish. In a large mixing bowl, combine flour, sugar and milk; pour over margarine, but do not mix. Add peaches; do not mix. Bake at 350 degrees for one hour. Makes 6 to 8 servings.

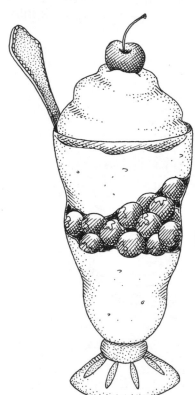

Quick treat!
Layer blueberries,
strawberry preserves and
vanilla ice cream in a parfait
glass. Top with whipped cream
and a cherry. Perfect for the
Fourth of July.

Angel's Delight

Carol Phillips
Seven Valleys, PA

If you don't care for peaches, try your favorite fruit.

6-oz. pkg. instant vanilla
   pudding mix
1 baked angel food cake, cubed

15-1/4 oz. can sliced peaches,
   drained
16 oz. whipped topping

Prepare pudding according to package directions; refrigerate for about 10 minutes. Line the bottom of a ungreased 13"x9" baking pan with angel food cake. Spread pudding over cake. Arrange peaches over top; spread whipped topping over all. Cover and refrigerate about one hour. Makes 18 to 24 servings.

Maple Pudding Cake

Sandy Andersen
Scotia, NY

Serve warm with whipped cream.

1-1/2 c. all-purpose flour
3/4 c. sugar
2 t. baking powder
1/4 t. salt

3/4 c. milk
1-1/2 c. maple syrup
3/4 c. water
2 T. butter

In a medium mixing bowl, combine flour, sugar, baking powder and salt; stir in milk. Spread mixture into a greased 9"x9" baking pan. In a medium saucepan, blend together remaining ingredients until butter is melted. Pour maple mixture over flour mixture. Bake at 350 degrees for 45 minutes. Makes 6 to 8 servings.

Simple Substitutions

Ingredient	Quantity	Substitutions
Baking Chocolate (Unsweetened)	1 square	1 T. shortening plus 3 T. cocoa
Baking Powder	1 t.	1/4 t. baking soda plus 1/2 t. cream of tartar
Baking Soda		no substitution
Broth, Chicken/Beef	1 c.	1 c. hot water plus 1 t. instant bouillon granules
Brown Sugar	1 c.	3/4 c. sugar plus 1/4 c. molasses
Butter	1 c.	1 c. margarine
Buttermilk	1 c.	1 c. milk less 1 T. plus 1 T. vinegar
Cake Flour	1 c.	1 c. all-purpose flour less 2 T.
Chocolate	1 oz.	3 T. cocoa plus 1 T. shortening
Chocolate, German	4 oz.	1/4 c. unsweetened cocoa plus 1/3 c. sugar and 3 T. oil
Cornstarch (for thickening)	1 T.	2 T. all-purpose flour
Cream of Tartar		no substitution
Dry Mustard	1 t.	1 T. prepared mustard
Garlic	1 clove	1/8 t. garlic powder
Herbs	1 T. fresh	1 t. dried
Honey	1 c.	1 c. molasses
Light Cream	1 c.	3 T. butter plus 7/8 c. milk
Milk	1 c.	1/2 c. evaporated milk plus 1/2 c. water
Molasses	1 c.	1 c. honey
Onion	1 c.	1 T. onion powder
Prepared Mustard	1 T.	1 t. dry mustard plus 2 t. vinegar

Ingredient	Quantity	Substitutions
Ricotta Cheese	1 c.	1 c. cottage cheese plus 1 T. skim milk
Self-Rising Flour	1 c.	1 c. all-purpose flour plus 1-1/2 t. baking powder and 1/2 t. salt
Sour Cream	1 c.	1 c. plain yogurt
Sour Milk	1 c.	1 c. milk less 1 T. plus 1 T. lemon juice
Tomato Sauce	1 c.	3/4 c. tomato paste plus 1 c. water
Whipping Cream	1 c.	1/3 c. butter plus 3/4 c. milk
Wine (for desserts)	1/2 c.	1/2 c. fruit juice
Wine (for cooking)	1/2 c.	1/2 c. chicken broth
Yogurt	1 c.	1 c. buttermilk

Measurements

pinch= 1/8 teaspoon
dash= 1/16 teaspoon
60 drops = 1 teaspoon
1 jigger = 3 tablespoons
3 teaspoons = 1 tablespoons
2 tablespoons = 1/8 cup
4 tablespoons = 1/4 cup

8 tablespoons = 1/2 cup
16 tablespoons = 1 cup
4 ounces = 1/2 cup
8 ounces = 1 cup
2 cups = 1 pint
4 cups = 1 quart
4 quarts = 1 gallon

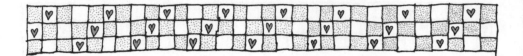

Herb Substitutions

Basil......oregano or thyme
Chervil......green onion
Cilantro.....parsley
Italian Seasoning......basil, oregano, rosemary and red pepper
Marjoram.....basil, thyme, or savory
Mint.....basil, marjoram, or rosemary
Oregano....thyme or basil
Poultry Seasoning.....sage, thyme, marjoram, savory, pepper and
    rosemary
Red Pepper.....hot pepper sauce
Rosemary.....thyme, tarragon, or savory
Sage.....savory, marjoram or rosemary
Tarragon....chervil
Thyme....oregano or marjoram

Spice Substitutions

Allspice....cinnamon, nutmeg, or mace
Aniseed....fennel seed or anise extract
Cardamom....ginger
Chili Powder....hot pepper sauce
Cinnamon.....nutmeg or allspice
Cloves....allspice, cinnamon, or nutmeg
Cumin.....chili powder
Ginger....allspice, cinnamon, mace, or nutmeg
Mace....allspice, cinnamon, ginger, or nutmeg
Nutmeg.....cinnamon, ginger, or mace
Saffron.....tumeric

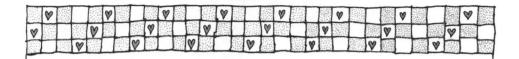

Equivalents

Apples	3 medium	3-1/2 cups, sliced
Bananas	3 medium	2 to 2-1/2 cups, sliced
Beans, dried kidney	2-1/3 cups	9 cups, cooked
Bread	1 slice	1/4 cup dry bread crumbs
Bread	1 slice	3/4 cup soft bread crumbs
Butter	1 stick	8 tablespoons or 1/2 cup
Cabbage	1 pound	3 cups, shredded
Carrots	8 to 10	2-3/4 cup, sliced
Celery	2 bunches	4 cups, diced
Chicken	3-1/2 pounds	2 cups, cooked and diced
Cream Cheese	3 ounces	6 tablespoons
Flour	1 pound	4 cups
Garlic	1 clove	1/4 teaspoon, chopped
Graham Crackers	15	1 cup finely crumbled
Lemon	1 medium	3 tablespoons juice
Macaroni	1 cup, uncooked	2 cups, cooked
Meat	1 pound	2 cups, diced
Mushrooms	1/2 pound	2-1/2 cups, sliced
Onions	1 medium	1/3 cup, chopped
Orange	1 medium	1/3 cup juice
Potatoes	3 medium	2-1/2 cups, sliced or 2 cups, mashed
Rice	1 cup, uncooked	3 cups, cooked
Spaghetti	1 pound, uncooked	7 cups, cooked
Sugar	1 pound	2 cups
Sugar, Brown	1 pound	2-3/4 cups
Tomatoes	4 medium	1-1/2 cups, chopped
Wafers, Vanilla	22 wafers	1 cup crumbled

Index

MMM

Homemade ♥

Sweet & simple

Index

a pinch & a dash

Yum

Index

so easy

Send us your favorite recipe!

and the memory that makes it special for you!* If we select your recipe for a brand-new **Gooseberry Patch** cookbook, your name will appear right along with it...and you'll receive a FREE copy of the book.

Share your recipe on our website at
www.gooseberrypatch.com

Or mail to:

Gooseberry Patch • Attn: Cookbook Dept.
PO Box 812 • Columbus, OH 43216-0812

*Don't forget to include your name, address, phone number and email address so we'll know how to reach you for your FREE book!

Since 1992, we've been publishing country cookbooks for every kitchen and for every meal of the day! Each has hundreds of budget-friendly recipes, using ingredients you already have on hand. Their lay-flat binding makes them easy to use and each is filled with hand-drawn artwork and plenty of personality.

Have a taste for more?

Call us toll-free at
1•800•854•6673

Find us here too!

We created our official **Circle of Friends** so we could fill everyone in on the latest scoop at once. Visit us online to join in the fun and discover free recipes, exclusive giveaways and much more!

www.gooseberrypatch.com

Email

U.S. to Metric Recipe Equivalents

Volume Measurements

1/4 teaspoon	1 mL
1/2 teaspoon	2 mL
1 teaspoon	5 mL
1 tablespoon = 3 teaspoons	15 mL
2 tablespoons = 1 fluid ounce	30 mL
1/4 cup	60 mL
1/3 cup	75 mL
1/2 cup = 4 fluid ounces	125 mL
1 cup = 8 fluid ounces	250 mL
2 cups = 1 pint =16 fluid ounces	500 mL
4 cups = 1 quart	1 L

Weights

1 ounce	30 g
4 ounces	120 g
8 ounces	225 g
16 ounces = 1 pound	450 g

Oven Temperatures

300° F	150° C
325° F	160° C
350° F	180° C
375° F	190° C
400° F	200° C
450° F	230° C

Baking Pan Sizes

Square		Loaf	
8x8x2 inches	2 L = 20x20x5 cm	9x5x3 inches	2 L = 23x13x7 cm
9x9x2 inches	2.5 L = 23x23x5 cm	Round	
Rectangular		8x1-1/2 inches	1.2 L = 20x4 cm
13x9x2 inches	3.5 L = 33x23x5 cm	9x1-1/2 inches	1.5 L = 23x4 cm